WEDDING LITURGIES

D0063972

Flor McCarthy is a Salesian priest who has worked as acatechist for many years in Dublin and has extensive parish experience in the U.S.A. as well as in Ireland. He is well known for his *Sunday and Holy Day Liturgies* and for *Funeral Liturgies*.

Wedding Liturgies

Flor McCarthy SDB

DOMINICAN PUBLICATIONS
COSTELLO PUBLISHING COMPANY

First published (1989) by
Dominican Publications
42 Parnell Square,
Dublin 1, Ireland.

ISBN 0-907271-96-0

American edition published by
Costello Publishing Company Inc.
P. O. Box 9, Northport,
Long Island, NY 11768, USA

Design by
Eddie McManus

Acknowledgements
Extracts from the Psalms are from *The Psalms: A New Translation*, published by William
Collins and Sons, and copyright The Grail, England.
   All other biblical passages are from the Revised Standard Version of the Bible, copy-
righted 1966 by the Division of Christian Education of the National Council of the
Churches of Christ in the USA.

Contents

Introduction

Scarcely any human enterprise is started with such high expectations, and so regularly fails to live up to those expectations, as marriage. Most couples enter marriage with sky-high expectations. They expect to be provided with continuous friendship and unwavering love.

Even though we know that these expectations are not only unrealistic but also impossible, it would be wrong to shoot them down, especially on a couple's wedding day. It would be unpardonable to throw cold water on their idealism or to dim in the slightest way the bright lamp of their hopes. The idealism with which young couples enter marriage is a perennial source of hope for the world.

What we are called to do is celebrate this idealism. Nevertheless, it ought to be possible to temper it with a little bit of realism by at least hinting at the patient work and willing sacrifice required to make their hopes and dreams come true. Thoreau gives us an example of how this might be done when he says, "If you have built castles in the air, your work need not be lost; that is where castles should be. Now put the foundation under them."

Today a lot of emphasis is placed on marriage as a relationship, and this is a good thing. God made us for community, not for the solitary life. We all pine for human warmth, closeness, and love. However, these things cannot be got from shallow and transient attachments, but only from deep and permanent relationships such as marriage.

In the eyes of the Church, when a couple get married they take an irreversible step, a step which has enormous consequences for them. They link their entire futures together. From this day forward their lives and destinies will be inextricably bound up with one another. This is an enormous thing to do. It is a huge commitment to make.

Marriage as a deep and loving relationship, the irreversible nature of the step taken, and the depth of the commitment involved — these are some of the topics which come in for special emphasis in these liturgies. When one considers how lightly some couples enter into marriage, and how frequently marriage ends in divorce, I think the attention given to them is well merited. I trust that the religious dimension of marriage is adequately catered for also.

All of this serves to underline the importance of the wedding ceremony. Alas, today the wedding ceremony is often the last thing the couple think about. The impression given is that it is something to be got over with so that the real thing can begin, namely, the reception. We must combat this tendency. We must do our utmost to help the couple to appreciate the importance of the ceremony. The Scripture readings have a vital part to play. Scripture illuminates well the decisive moments in the life of a Christian. The Word of God sheds marvellous light into the nature and meaning of marriage.

It is customary nowadays that the couple choose their own readings. This is good, but often the choice is rather a hit and miss affair. The average couple needs a little help. The very least we can do is provide them with a rich menu to choose from.

I have suggested a set of readings for each of the liturgies here, and for convenience these are included in the book. However, the selection is by no means exhaustive. As far as possible each set contains one reading which deals with the divine origin of marriage, and one which deals with the place of love in the life of the Christian. I believe these two elements are very important. This is something the couple might keep in mind when making their choice.

For many priests the homily is their main, if not only, concern. This is a pity. The whole liturgy is important, and every part of it speaks. Hence, I have provided not just wedding homilies but wedding liturgies.

The homily should not be turned into a marriage instruction. The latter should have been taken care of in the pre-marriage talks and/or course. The homily should shed light on the meaning of marriage, and at the same time provide inspiration and hope. It gives us a chance to talk about the heart of the Gospel — God's love for us and our love for one another.

There are some who maintain that it doesn't matter what you say in the homily because the couple will be so nervous, excited and distracted that they won't hear it. No doubt there is some truth in this, but at the same time we shouldn't underestimate them.

Even if it were one hundred per cent true, one's words would still not be wasted. There will be plenty of other couples present who will hear what is said and benefit from it. People are usually very receptive on occasions such as this. The fact that the homily is not aimed directly at them makes it even more effective.

The heart of the ceremony is, of course, the exchange of vows. We must do everything in our power to highlight and solemnize this moment. It must be made clear that the couple are the ministers of the sacrament. Hence, the presiding minister should step into the background at this point so as to allow the bride and groom to occupy the centre of the stage. The bestman and bridesmaid must also be helped to play their full part in this moment.

Most times the ceremony includes the celebration of the Eucharist. Sometimes, however, it does not. Both possibilities are taken into account in the book.

Four liturgies for wedding anniversaries, as well as a formula for the renewal of the wedding vows, are also provided. Included also are a number of reflections which can be used to good effect.

There is a lot of concern today about the secular nature of some of the music which is being used at wedding ceremonies. What is proposed is often not a hymn but a secular song more suited to the wedding reception than the church service. This practice should be discouraged. The fact that it is done with the best of intentions makes no difference.

Weddings provide a marvellous pastoral opportunity. We must be positive in what we say, but especially in what we do. When all is said and done, it is not the words we address to the couple, no matter how inspiring those words may be, that matter. What matters is how we treat the couple, that we be as kind and helpful as we possibly can lest we tarnish the joy of this unique day in their lives. How we treat them is what they will remember long after our words have faded into the night of oblivion.

Flor McCarthy

To enter marriage
is to enter a school of love.

FYODOR DOSTOYEVSKY

Liturgies

1. WHERE LOVE IS, GOD IS

Introduction

In the name of the Father and of the Son and of the Holy Spirit. The Lord be with you.

Today N. and N. come before God and this community to declare their love for each other and to celebrate it. We know that God is present in their love, because where love is, God is.

Love comes from God. He loves each of us without distinction. Besides, he has made a covenant of love with his people, the Church, and he is faithful to this covenant forever.

Wedding Ceremony without Mass

Let us reflect for a moment on God's love for us, a love which he bestows on us irrespective of whether we are worthy. [*Pause*].

Opening Prayer

Let us pray:
Heavenly Father, we know that you love us and want us to love one another. Hear our prayers for N. and N., who today are united in marriage. Help them so to love one another that they will always experience your loving presence in their lives. We ask this through Christ our Lord.

Wedding within Mass

Penitential Rite

God wants us to love one another. For followers of Christ the only real failure is the failure to love. Let us reflect for a moment on our failure to love others as we should. [*Pause*]

Now let us turn to the Lord who forgives our sins and helps us to love one another.

Lord, you came to teach us how to love our heavenly Father with all our heart and all our soul. Lord, have mercy.

You came to teach us how to love our neighbour as ourselves. Christ, have mercy.

You came to teach us that these two commandments sum up the whole of religion. Lord, have mercy.

Opening Prayer

Cf. Roman Missal

Readings on page 78.

Homily

Love is the most powerful force in the world. It calls forth the greatest sacrifices, leads to the deepest commitment, and forges an unbreakable bond between people. The truth of this is well illustrated in the following story.

Once in a certain kingdom lived two men who made a vow to be friends till death. "Nothing will part us," they declared. Fine words, brave words, yet easily said. The question is: did they really mean them?

Well, those words were soon put to the test. One of them was accused of being involved in subversive activities. He was arrested and imprisoned. What did the other do? Without a moment's hesitation, he came to the aid of his friend, and insisted on taking the blame on himself. The result was that both were brought to trial. But they remained loyal to one another in court, so that the judge was hopelessly confused.

The case attracted nationwide attention. Finally it reached the ears of the king himself. He ordered the two men to be brought before him.

"We're for it now," the friends said to one another.

However, they were in for a delightful surprise. The king received them warmly and said to them, "You've nothing to worry about. I'm going to set you both free. But before I do so I have a favour to ask of you."

"A favour, your Majesty! What favour could two poor men do for a king?" they asked in astonishment.

"I want you to take me as the third partner in your friendship," the king replied.

Naturally the two were only too happy to agree to the king's surprising request.

Here we see two people who sealed their friendship with a solemn vow. No one forced them to make this vow. It sprang entirely from the pure and unselfish love they had for one another. And the vow they made was not just a matter of words. They were prepared to back it up with deeds, indeed with their very lives if necessary.

What those two friends did was truly extraordinary. Yet what N. and N. are doing is every bit as extraordinary. They are pledging their love in marriage. However, we are so familiar with marriage that we don't always appreciate the depth of commitment it involves. When a man and woman get married they make a solemn vow to be true to one another till death. This vow is not a private one but a public one. They do so of their own free will. Why do they make this vow? Because they love one another, or if you like, because they are friends and want to seal their friendship forever.

Love is not only a powerful thing, but also a holy thing. Love comes from God. What a wonderful statement St John made about God, when he said, "God is love." It follows that where love is, God is. Hence, when two people truly love one another, then God himself becomes their partner. When two people commit themselves to one another, God commits himself with them.

The solemn pledge of love which N. and N. are about to make to each other, and which will be sealed in the sacrament of matrimony, is as yet largely a matter of words. But these words will have to be translated into deeds, because their pledge is certain to be tested, not once, but many times, in the course of their life together. But God is their partner in this adventure of love. Let them remember this, and have recourse to him, when things are difficult.

God puts his seal on their friendship and on the bond by which they bind their lives and destinies on this red-letter day in their (young) lives., He blesses their love and wants it to bear fruit, fruit that will remain.

"Learning to love is hard and we pay dearly for it. To enter marriage is to enter a school of love." (Dostoyevsky).

"The opposite to love is not hate but indifference." (Elie Wiesel).

Prayer of the Faithful

President: Let us pray that we may be able to love, since God is love, and love comes from him. Those who love, know God, and experience his presence in their lives.

Response: Lord, hear our prayer.

Reader(s): For all the followers of Christ: that they may be witnesses to his love by the concern they show for one another. Let us pray to the Lord.

For world leaders: that they may work without ceasing to build a more just and human world. Let us pray to the Lord.

For N. and N., now married in Christ: that this Christian marriage, which has begun in joy, may endure in peace. Let us pray to the Lord.

That in the midst of the difficulties and challenges of life they may remain true and loyal friends to one another. Let us pray to the Lord.

For all here present: that they may be inspired by the love of N. and N., and so find strength to persevere in their efforts to love others unselfishly. Let us pray to the Lord.

For the lonely and the unloved: that they may find comfort and support. Let us pray to the Lord.

President: Heavenly Father, by the grace of the Holy Spirit you pour into our hearts the ability to love. Grant a generous increase of this gift to this couple, to their families, and to the whole Christian community. We ask this through Christ our Lord.

(Communion) Reflection

No. 4 or No. 7.

2. LOVE IS ... *I*

Introduction

In the name of the Father and of the Son and of the Holy Spirit.
The grace of our Lord Jesus Christ, the love of God, and the fellowship of the Holy Spirit be with you all.

If you had a fruit tree in your garden which never produced any fruit, then, no matter how tall, full of leaves, and impressive to look at it might be, you wouldn't think it much of a fruit tree.

A human being who is unable to love, even though rich in material possessions and other qualities, is no better than a barren fruit tree. Love is the one fruit that makes us rich as human beings and children of God.

Wedding Ceremony without Mass

Let us reflect on this for a moment. [*Pause*]

God wants us to love one another. To this end he has given each of us the gift to love. Let us ask him to help us to make good use of this gift. Let us ask him especially to help and bless N. and N., who today commit themselves to one another in love.

Opening Prayer

Let us pray:

Father, we know it is your will that we should love one another. But we also know that without your help we are unable to love as we should. Look with kindness on N. and N., who today solemnly pledge to love one another for life. Touch their hearts and strengthen their wills so that they may be capable of true and lasting love. We ask this through Christ our Lord.

Wedding within Mass

Penitential Rite

Of all the commandments Christ gave us, the commandment to love is the most important. "Love one another as I have loved you," he said. This sums up everything.

Hence, the only failure in the life of a disciple of Christ is the failure to love. Let us pause for a moment to reflect on the fact that we do not love others as we should. [*Pause*]

Let us now confess our sins, especially those against the commandment to love.

I confess to almighty God.

Opening Prayer

Cf. Roman Missal

Readings on page 80.

Homily

One day a beggarman made the rounds of a village but got nothing. Weary and dejected he sat down by the side of the road. At his side lay a sack which contained a handful of wheat. In the evening he would grind it down and bake a last cake of bread.

Suddenly, however, he saw the king's carriage approaching. "The king is a kind man. He will surely give me something," said the beggar to himself, as he jumped to his feet. To his delight the royal carriage came to a halt directly opposite the spot where he stood with outstretched hand.

Down came the window of the carriage and the king appeared. The beggarman was about to say, "Your Majesty, could you spare a little money for your unworthy servant?" But the king got in the first words. Reaching out an empty hand he said, "Friend, could you spare a little corn for your king?"

Completely taken aback, the beggarman said, "Certainly, your Majesty." With that he opened the sack, picked out the smallest grain he could find, and gave it to the king. The king thanked him and the carriage moved off.

On arriving home that evening the beggarman emptied the last of his wheat into a pan. As he inspected the miserable little heap of grains that resulted, he make a startling discovery. The smallest grain had turned into a grain of pure gold. Then he bitterly regretted that he had been so miserly with his king.

It is not in receiving but in giving that we are enriched. However, there is true giving and false giving. False giving inflates the ego of the giver, and keeps the receiver in a state of dependence. True giving, on the other hand, is a selfless thing, and seeks to set the receiver free.

It would have been easy for the king to give some money to the beggarman. Had he done so he would have enhanced his standing in front of his entourage. But what would it have done for the beggar? It would have made him happy for a day, but next day he would be as badly off as ever.

The greatest good we can do for another person is not to give him of our own wealth but rather to show him his own. Thus, by asking something from the beggar, the king showed that he regarded. him as a worthwhile person who had "riches" to share with others, riches fit even for a king. Unfortunately the beggar didn't see it like this. He saw giving as losing something.

Many people are afraid of giving because they see it as being deprived of something. But this need not be so. A tree grows, not simply by receiving from nature, but by putting out buds and shoots. To give is to enhance one's life. Genuine love enlarges rather than diminishes us. Love awakens energies and resources in us we never knew were there. To close one's heart is to begin to die. To open one's heart is to begin to live.

Nothing provides such opportunities for giving as marriage. However, many come to marriage with the mentality of a beggar. They want to receive and take, but not to give. In a poll a number of people were asked, "Why do you want to get married?" Almost all replied, "To be loved." One fears for marriages that begin like this, because those who take from others are never satisfied.

On the other hand, when you have a couple who are willing to give as well as to receive, there is great hope for their marriage. Love is kept by giving it away, but it can only be given perfectly when it is also received. Love given and received brings out the best in us. This is why marriage provides such opportunities for growth.

N. and N. are about to pledge their love for one another in the sacrament of matrimony. May the Lord help them so to give and receive love, that they will not only have a happy life together, but also reach their full potential as human beings and as his precious children.

"If you want to be happy, give without counting or regrets." (Michel Quoist).

"A man's wealth consists not in what he keeps but in what he gives away." (Rabbinical saying).

Prayer of the Faithful

President: God the Father wants us to love one another. He sent his Son among us to give us an example of unselfish love and to remind us that our true vocation in life is to be loving people. Let us pray for the ability to love.

Response: Lord, hear us in your love.

Reader(s): For all the followers of Christ: that their love for one another may be sincere and practical. We pray in faith.

For world leaders: that through goodwill and cooperation they may put an end to war and hunger. We pray in faith.

For N. and N., who have committed themselves to one another in love: that the Lord may keep them true and faithful to one another. We pray in faith.

That God may bless their love and make it fruitful so that it may enrich their lives and the lives of others. We pray in faith.

For all here present: that we may not be content merely to love our friends, but reach out also to those who make life difficult for us. We pray in faith.

For those who do not know how to love because they never received love. We pray in faith.

President: Heavenly Father, you are our source of life. You know our weakness. May we reach out with trust to grasp your hand so that we may be able to walk joyfully and courageously in the ways of love. We ask this through Christ our Lord.

(Communion) Reflection

No. 2 or No. 1.

3. LOVE IS ... *II*

Introduction

In the name of the Father and of the Son and of the Holy Spirit.
The grace and peace of God our Father and the Lord Jesus Christ be with you.

We are gathered here today to celebrate love, first and foremost God's love for us in Christ. "God loved the world so much that he gave his only Son, so that everyone who believes in him may not be lost but may have eternal life." (John 3:16). This is a cause of great joy and hope for us.

But today we are also celebrating our love for one another, and of course especially the love of N. and N. for each other. St Paul says, "If I have not love, I am nothing." That's how vital love is. The person who does not love is like a lamp that does not give light.

Wedding Ceremony without Mass

Let us reflect for a moment on the importance of love in human life, and especially in the life of a Christian. [*Pause*]

Opening Prayer

Let us pray:
Father, we know that when we love others we pass from death to life. Look with love on N. and N., who today are united in the sacrament of marriage. Cleanse their hearts from all selfishness, so that their love for one another may be true and constant. We ask this through Christ our Lord.

Wedding within Mass

Penitential Rite

Let us pause to call to mind our failures to love. [*Pause*] In this Eucharist we experience Christ's forgiveness and acceptance.

Lord, you reveal to us the Father's unconditional love for us. Lord, have mercy.

You gave us the greatest possible proof of love when you laid down your life for us. Christ, have mercy.

You want us to love one another so that our lives may be happy and fruitful. Lord, have mercy.

Opening Prayer

Cf. Roman Missal

Readings on page 82.

Homily

We are gathered here to celebrate love, the love of N. and N. for each other. Basically there are two kinds of love — selfish love and unselfish love. The former brings death, the latter brings life. One of Aesop's fables gives an example of selfish love in action. It goes as follows.

One day a lonely, unloved child was sitting by a wall when a toad emerged from a cave close by. In a flash the child took out her silk scarf — the kind which toads love to walk on — and spread it out before him. As soon as the toad saw the scarf he went back into the cave, and soon returned carrying a little crown of gold which he laid on the scarf. Then he went into the cave again.

On seeing the glittering crown, the child's eyes lit up with desire. She reached out and grabbed it. After examining it for a while, she put it into her pocket. Soon the toad came out again, but when he didn't see the crown on the scarf, he crept over to the wall, and from sheer sorrow at discovering that he had been robbed of his treasure, beat his little head against the wall until he fell dead.

That child didn't love the toad. Far from loving him, she cruelly exploited him. She saw that he had something desirable. Without a thought for the feelings of the poor little fellow, she took it. She acted not only very selfishly but foolishly as well, because had she been patient, and let the crown lie where it was, she would have had the joy of watching the toad bring out more of his treasures from the cave.

Selfish love uses the other person for its own gain. The attitude, which may be completely unconscious, is: the other person exists for me. This, of course, is not love at all but the worst form of selfishness. Selfish love diminishes us and is very damaging to the other person. It causes the other person to close up and acts as a blight on his (her) generosity.

Unselfish love, on the other hand, helps the other to unfold. It does everything in its power to encourage the other to come out of "the cave" and share his (her) "treasures" with the world. It has no desire to take possession of those treasures. It accepts them if offered, but it wouldn't dream of plundering them. It shows an active concern for the happiness, growth, and life of the loved one.

Sometimes when two people fall in love they desire rather than love each other. Desire , however, is only a starting point. It may lead to love, but it is not love. If there is not concern for the other person, but only a desire to receive, to possess, then what results is not love but exploitation. Love goes beyond desire. Those who stop at desire will never know love. When they have taken all they want, they will begin to look elsewhere for another desire and another fulfilment.

Of ourselves we are incomplete. Hence, we need to receive from others. But if we wish to love we have to got beyond not only the desire to take, but even the desire to receive from the other, and want to give. We need to come out of the cave of selfishness and open ourselves to the other. There is a risk involved, because when we do this, like the little toad, we are putting our treasures on display. But the alternative is to crawl back into our cave and shrivel up.

We all are capable of love, but our love is not pure. It is tainted with selfishness. We need to ask the Lord to purify our hearts so that our love will be unspoilt. However, this kind of love is not something which will be given to us overnight. It may take a lifetime to acquire it.

May the Lord, who loves us with a pure and unfailing love, help N. and N. to love one another in such a way that they will be able to share the treasures of their goodness with one another.

"The prevailing philosophy is: everything must be grabbed from life immediately and with both hands." (Solzhenitsyn).

"Love is the greatest of all risks."(Jean Vanier).

Prayer of the Faithful

President: If we have faith strong enough to move mountains, but are without love, we are nothing at all. Mindful of these words of St Paul, let us pray to God for the gift of true love.

Response: Lord, grant us the gift of love.

Reader(s): For the Church: that it may never forget the primacy of love, and never tire in urging its members to love one another. Let us pray in faith.

For world leaders: that they may work untiringly to build a world free from poverty and oppression, so that all peoples may be able to live in freedom and dignity. Let us pray in faith.

For N. and N.: that the Lord may strengthen their love for one another, and purify it from all traces of self-seeking. Let us pray in faith.

That they may be able to give to one another with constancy and generosity, and to receive from one another with humility and graciousness. Let us pray in faith.

For all of us who are celebrating with them today: that this day may bring us blessings, and encourage us to be constant and faithful in love. Let us pray in faith.

For those who have died: that the Lord's eternal love and mercy may shine brightly on them. Let us pray in faith.

President: God, our Father, you are the same yesterday, today, and forever. Help us to have confidence in your unchanging love for us, so that when things are difficult we may have the strength to persevere in the way of love. We ask this through Christ our Lord.

(Communion) Reflection
No. 1 or No. 2.

4. THE LAMP OF LOVE

Introduction

In the name of the Father and of the Son and of the Holy Spirit.
The Lord be with you.

The term "love" has become somewhat devalued. This is a pity because love is as necessary for us as light. In fact it is a special kind of light. Without it our lives would be very dark indeed. Those who love are living in broad daylight. Those who do not love are in deep darkness.

This is a bright day for N. and N. It is a bright day for all of us. Thanks to their love, a new lamp shines in our midst. We are happy for them. We are also grateful to them.

Wedding Ceremony without Mass

But we know that the lamp of human love is at best frail and unreliable. It can grow dim or even go out altogether. The one lamp that never goes out or grows dim is the lamp of God's love for us. In God there is no shadow or trace of darkness.

Let us turn to him and ask him to help us, and particularly N. and N., to walk in the light of faithful love. [*Pause*]

Opening Prayer

Let us pray:
Heavenly Father, to live in love is to live in the light. Let the light of your love shine brightly on N. and N., who today are being united in the sacrament of marriage. Bless their love. May its unwavering flame enable them to walk with confidence and hope through the shadows of this world until they reach your homeland of endless day. We ask this through Christ our Lord.

Wedding within Mass

Penitential Rite

The lamp of human love is at best frail and unreliable. We need the light which comes from Christ and his Gospel, a light which shines for all those who belive in him and follow him. Let us turn to him now, and ask forgiveness for the darkness we bring into our own lives and the lives of others. [*Pause*]

Lord, through the light of faith you help us to banish the shadows of doubt and unbelief. Lord, have mercy.

Through the light of hope you help us to banish the shadows of sadness and despair. Christ, have mercy.

Through the light of love you help us to banish the shadows of indifference and hostility. Lord, have mercy.

Opening Prayer

Cf. Roman Missal

Readings on page 85.

Homily

This liturgy involves the use of two small candles and one large one. One of the small candles stands for the love of the bride; the other for the love of the groom. The large candle stands for the "lamp" of their married love which is put on public display on this day.

The two small candles are lighting from the start of the ceremony. The large one is lit after the couple have exchanged their vows. This is a very simple ritual yet it communicates powerfully. The fewer words of explanation the better. When performed well it will speak for itself.

Light is a beautiful and wonderful thing. It is also a powerful symbol. It can stand for many things — truth, hope, joy, and so on. In this ceremony we are going to use it as a symbol of love. Light then stands for love. Darkness stands for the opposite to love. Anyone who loves is in the light. Anyone who does not love is in darkness.

Love is much-abused term. Therefore it would be easy to be cynical about it. But the truth is, without love the world would be a very dark place. Without love our lives would be enveloped in gloom. Love lights up everything. It brings hope to a world filled with the shadows of selfishness, indifference and hatred.

When you meet a truly loving person you notice that there is a brightness about him (her) which shines in the face, and especially in the eyes. Those who love shed light around them because love makes everything bright. Love brings out the best in the lover. People are at their best and brightest when loving. They are like a glowing lamp.

Each of us has an innate, great capacity to love. The Bible states that we are make in God's image. The image of God is at its best and brightest in us when we love. When we love we become like God, who as St John said, is love. Each of us, therefore, is capable of shedding light, if not into the world at large, at least into our own immediate environment.

I've no doubt but that N. and N. have a lot of love in them. This means they are capable of shedding a lot of light into each other's lives. The two (small) candles that are lighting on the altar stand for their individual loves. For some time now these lights have been burning quietly and , to some extent, secretly. Very soon N. and N. will take their individual candles and with they they will light the large candle. Thus they will publicly proclaim the joining of their lives, and the sharing of the light of their love with one another.

Today their lives come together. Though they do not lose their individuality, nevertheless, marriage unites them in so close a union that in a sense they become one. From now on their light will shine for one another. And not just for one another. Today, just as Christ wished, through the ministry of the Church, they are placing the lamp of their love on a lamp-stand. Thus it will give light, not only to them, but to their families, friends, the community, and to an extent to all the world. This is a happy day. The whole Church rejoices with them.

Thanks to technology, today we have lamps that never go out. The human lamp, however, hasn't changed much over the centuries. It is still a frail and imperfect thing. This is so because we have within us a certain amount of darkness. Our innate selfishness dims the lamp of love. We also have to contend with the darkness which is in others and in the world at large. N. and N. will, therefore, need to take good care of this precious lamp to ensure that it will go on burning brightly.

Above all they will need the help of Christ in order to believe in love and go on giving it to one another with generosity and constancy. Christ showed an undying love for us, his brothers and sisters. Sent by the Father into the world, he was "the true light of the world". And to those who believe in him and follow him he made a marvellous promise. He promised that they would never walk in darkness but would always have the light of life.

Happy, then, N. and N. if they have faith in Christ and seek his help through prayer and the sacraments. When the lamp of their love grows dim, Christ's light will show them the way and lead them forward.

"Where there is love there is pain." (Catherine de Hueck Doherty).

"The tragedy of man is that he doesn't know how to distinguish between day and night." (Elie Wiesel).

Prayer of the Faithful

President: We have lifted up the lamp of love and placed it on the lampstand so that it can give light to all here present. Let us turn to God to ask his blessing on us all, and especially on N. and N.

Response: Let your light shine on us, O Lord.

Reader(s): For the Church: that through its ministry the light of the Gospel may shine for all the world to see. Let us pray.

For the world in which we live, a world darkened by war and want. Let us pray.

For N. and N. : that they may always walk in the light of true love. Let us pray.

That the darkness of human weakness and sinfulness may not cause them to stumble or lose their way. Let us pray.

For those who have never known the warmth and brightness of love, and who have had to live out their lives in the shadows of apathy and neglect. Let us pray.

For all here present: that this celebration may encourage us to persevere in the way of love. Let us pray.

That God's light may shine gently on our departed loved ones. Let us pray.

President: Heavenly Father, may the radiance of your love light up our hearts, and bring us safely through the shadows of this world until we reach our homeland of everlasting light. We ask this through Christ our Lord.

(Communion) Reflection

No. 12 or No. 7.

5. WHEN THE WINE RUNS OUT

Introduction

In the name of the Father and of the Son and of the Holy Spirit.

The grace of our Lord Jesus Christ, the love of God, and the fellowship of the Holy Spirit be with you all.

Though water has no taste, colour, or smell, it is a miracle. Without it there would be no life on earth. Yet no one in his right mind would compare it to wine. Strictly speaking we could survive without wine, but life would be the poorer for its absence.

Wine is a symbol of love. We could survive without love, but how bleak our lives would be if we never tasted its wine.

At Cana Jesus changed water into excellent wine. He is present with us today as we celebrate the wedding of N. and N. Married people especially need to be able to give and receive the wine of love. A marriage without love is like a wedding feast without wine.

Wedding Ceremony without Mass

Let us pause to reflect on this, and to enliven our faith in the loving presence of Christ among us. [*Pause*]

Opening Prayer

Let us pray:

Father, love is our highest calling. Hear our prayers for N. and N., who today are celebrating their marriage. May Christ who brought happiness to a wedding at Cana be present with them today and throughout their marriage. When through human weakness the wine of their love is found wanting, may he touch their hearts and strengthen their wills with his grace, so that they may taste the new wine of unselfish love. We ask this through the same Christ our Lord.

Wedding within Mass

Penitential Rite

Let us pause to reflect on how poor and inconsistent is the love we give to, and receive from, others. *[Pause]* In our poverty let us seek the help of Christ with confidence.

Lord, you help us to change the water of doubt into the wine of faith. Lord, have mercy.

You help us to change the water of despair into the wine of hope. Christ, have mercy.

You help us the change the water of selfishness into the wine of love. Lord, have mercy.

Opening Prayer

Cf. Roman Missal.

Readings on page 88.

Homily

What happened at Cana happens sooner or later in every marriage, namely, the wine runs out. What does this mean?

Hardly any enterprise is started with such high expectations as marriage. The average marriage beings with a feast of joy. The couple are surrounded by a host of friends who smother them with presents. Full of hopes and dreams, they set off on their honeymoon. The wine is flowing freely.

They come back from the honeymoon and the real business begins — setting up a home and learning to live with one another. At first they find great joy in each other's company. They are convinced that their love was pre-ordained in heaven and meant to last for eternity. It looks as if those expectations are going to be fulfilled. The wine is still flowing.

But when two human beings get close to one another inevitably problems occur. Tensions arise. The warts and cracks in each other begin to show up. They discover that they did not marry an angel after all, but a human being wounded by sin and selfishness. They are alarmed at the poverty they discover in one another. The honeymoon is over. The wine has run out. All that is left is the 'water' of their own meagre resources.

What should they do? Some panic and decide to run out with the wine. "There's nothing in it for me any longer," they say. "Therefore, I've decided to get out. I'm entitled to wine. No way am I going to settle for water."

While this attitude may sound reasonable it implies a great selfishness. Couples who act like this desire rather than love one another. For them marriage is but a passing alliance of two selfish human beings. When they have taken all they can from one another, they begin to look elsewhere for more fruit that can be picked without effort or pain.

But what can a couple do? For a start they should acknowledge that the first wine has run out. It is gone forever. For the moment they will have to make do with water. But here is a surprising thing. It is necessary that the first wine should run out. Otherwise how can the new wine come in?

So when it happens there is no need for panic or despair. They must hold on. They must also beware of looking for false substitutes, such as losing themselves in a career or in a hectic social life, and so on. That is, they must resist the temptation to abandon the relationship through which they can grow as persons and discover the real meaning of love. What they must do is begin in real earnest to work on the relationship.

First love, or romantic love as it's called, cannot last. It is bound to wear out. But this is not a tragedy. It is a necessity. It has to wear out so that a new and deeper love can be born, just as the blossoms have to die so that the fruit can come. The new love is typified by Mary's attitude at Cana — "they have no wine". In other words, it consists in putting the other person before ourselves. We have to forget ourselves and find our joy in loving rather than in being loved, in giving rather than in receiving. True love seeks only on thing — the good of the loved one.

Love is an exacting and difficult adventure. To enter marriage is to enter a school of love, a school in which we all are slow learners. It requires a lot of effort to go from a desire to receive to a desire to give. It is impossible to unaided human nature. This is why, like the couple of Cana, we need the presence of Christ.

When N. and N. come up against their limitations they know who to turn to. Christ touches our hearts and helps us to love unselfishly. For those with faith in him the miracle of Cana still happens — the water of selfishness is turned into the wine of true love. And wonderful as the old wine was, the new wine is still better.

"Real love begins where nothing is expected in return." (Antoine de Saint Exupery).

"Falling in love with someone doesn't mean loving that person."
(Dostoyevsky).

Prayer of the Faithful

President: Let us pray to God our Father that through his Son Jesus the
miracle of Cana may happen in our families, in our commu-
nities, and in the hearts of each of us.

Response: Lord, hear our prayer.

Reader(s): For the pope, bishops, and leaders of the Church: that they
may build it into a sacrament of unity, love and peace. Let us
pray to the Lord.

For all those who hold public office: that God may give them
a strong and unselfish love so that they may work for the
progress of all peoples. Let us pray to the Lord.

For N. and N., whose marriage we are celebrating: that they
may know the presence of Christ and his mother in their
married life, so that they may be able to change the water of
selfishness into the wine of pure love. Let us pray to the Lord.

For all married couples, especially those here present: that
Christ may help them to persevere when they experience their
own and their partner's poverty and human frailty. Let us pray
to the Lord.

For those who have never known the wine of love and joy in
their lives: that they too may experience the blessings of love.
Let us pray to the Lord.

Now in silence let each of us bring our needs before God.
[*Pause*] Let us pray to the Lord.

President: Heavenly Father, may we experience your Son's gentle and
loving presence in our lives, so that when our own efforts are
not enough, he may support us with his grace and strength. We
ask this through the same Christ our Lord.

(Communion) Reflection
No.6 or No.5.

6. GIVING ONE'S SOLEMN WORD

Introduction

In the name of the Father and of the Son and of the Holy Spirit.
The grace and peace of God our Father and the Lord Jesus Christ be with you.

This is truly a fateful day for N. and N. Today they are taking a decisive step. They are giving their word irrevocably to one another. The Church is happy for them and blesses them. We are happy for them and want to encourage and support them through our presence, prayers, and good wishes.

To be faithful and true to one's word is no easy matter. Marriage calls for the most profound fidelity of all. Fidelity demands discipline and sacrifice, things which never come easy. In truth, only one is truly and fully faithful to his word, and that is God. Though we may abandon him, he doesn't abandon us.

Wedding Ceremony without Mass

So let us turn to him with great confidence, asking him for the grace of fidelity for ourselves, and particularly for N. and N. [*Pause*]

Opening Prayer

Let us pray:
Father, you are always faithful to us, and guide us in all our decisions. Bless N. and N., who today give their solemn word to be faithful to one another in marriage. Support them in times of difficulty, save them from the darkness of broken promises, and help them to walk the bright path of faithful love. We ask this through Christ our Lord.

Wedding within Mass

Penitential Rite

So let us turn to him with confidence, asking his forgiveness for our infidelities, and the grace to be faithful and true. [*Pause*]

Lord, you are compassionate and loving, slow to anger and rich in mercy. Lord, have mercy.

You forgive all our sins; you heal every one of our ills. Christ, have mercy.

As a father has compassion on his children, so you have compassion on those who revere you. Lord, have mercy.

Opening Prayer

Cf. Roman Missal

Readings on page 90.

Homily

One of the greatest things we can give to another person is not a thing at all. It is a word. But it is easy to give a word. It doesn't cost anything there and then. The cost comes later. It's easy to take out a mortgage. Not so easy to keep up the repayments. And we possess only what we've paid for.

Some people are prodigal with their word. They'll promise you the sun, moon, and stars. But you can't rely on them. Their word is worthless. They don't really mean it. How painful it is to deal with such people.

But then there are other people who are quite frugal with their word. They do not make promises easily. But when they do make a promise you can be one hundred per cent sure that they will honour it. They are absolutely trustworthy. Their promise is like a chain around their leg. How lovely it is to deal with such people.

Faithfulness is one of the greatest and most necessary things in life. It is as precious as a gem, and almost as rare. "To be a human being is precisely to be faithful" (Antoine de Saint Exupery). But faithfulness is costly. It is not an easy road. It is a hard road. If one wishes to be faithful one must be prepared to put oneself, one's pleasures, comforts, and interests in second place.

Faithfulness is the ability to stick with one's choice, the will to struggle for it, and to turn the inevitable obstacles and set-backs into positive elements on one's chosen path. It requires not so much physical strength as strength of character. will and spirit. Though it is costly, even here on earth it brings great rewards in terms of joy, serenity and growth. There can be no happiness, no growth, except in the fulfilment of one's obligations. A person's moral greatness consists in faithfulness.

Today N. and N. are giving their word to one another. It is not just any word. It is a solemn word, a promise, a vow. They are giving it not just for a couple of years, but for life — "till death do us part". This means they are giving their word irrevocably to one another.

When you stop to think about it, what they are doing is quite enormous. They are making a life-long commitment to one another. This is something which must be done in complete freedom, and only after careful preparation and consideration. And what a risky thing it is they are doing — committing their whole lives to the slender thread of the word of another human being! The promises they are making call for a huge amount of mutual trust. Of course there is uncertainty. Of course there are doubts. But as trust grows this uncertainty and these doubts will disappear.

This a fateful day for them. They are giving their lives into each other's keeping. They not only vow to love each other forever, but intend to follow through on it — to live a long, full, and authentic life based on this vow. They are putting their allotted amount of precious time on this earth where their hearts are.

This is asking an awful lot of weak human beings. Those who have a sure faith are lucky, because another kind of strength becomes available to them. God is the only one who is truly and fully faithful to his word. Out of love for us he entered into a covenant of friendship with us in Christ. He has bound himself to us by a bond that can never be broken. He remains faithful to us in spite of halfheartedness, infidelity, and even rebelliousness on our part. He remains faithful because he loves us. Fidelity is rooted in love. Where true love exists, fidelity comes naturally and easily.

God looks with love on N. and N. today as they make this solemn covenant of love with one another. As yet their promises are only paper promises. But the Lord will confirm and seal them. Through the holy sacrament of matrimony his grace will become available to them. May he give them the grace of a genuine love for one another. Then fidelity will spring up like a flower in the garden of their love, and they can expect the greatest measure of happiness a man and woman can have.

God is with all those who ever decide to love each other faithfully.

"Faithfulness is an adventure, a way to be followed because it has been chosen" (Michel Quoist).

"When a man takes an oath he's holding his whole self in his hands, like a man who cups his hands and fills them with water. If he opens his fingers he mustn't hope to find himself again." (Thomas More).

Prayer of the Faithful

President: Let us pray to God our Father, who alone is totally faithful to his word, asking him to save us from the darkness of broken promises, and to help us to walk in the light of faithfulness and truth.

Response: Lord, graciously hear us.

Reader(s): For all Christians: that they may be steadfast in faith, joyful in hope, and untiring in love. Lord, hear us.

For all our political and civil leaders: that they may be faithful to their promises and commitments. Lord, hear us.

For N. and N.: that the Lord may help them to be true to the solemn promises they exchange on this joyful day. Lord, hear us.

That their youthful love may never wilt; rather that it may grow stronger as each year goes by. Lord, hear us.

For all married couples: that they may remain faithful to one another in spite of their own weakness and the difficulties of life. Lord, hear us.

For those who have been the victims of broken promises: that they may find healing and peace. Lord, hear us.

Now in silence let each of us place our own needs before God. [*Pause*] Lord, hear us.

President: Heavenly Father, help us to keep our hearts pure, our minds clean, our words true, and our deeds kind. We ask this through Christ our Lord

(Communion) Reflection

No. 11 or No. 15.

7. WHEN TWO ROADS MEET

Introduction

In the name of the Father and of the Son and of the Holy Spirit. The Lord be with you.

Married or single, we are all embarked on a great journey — the journey of life, a journey which leads to the fullness of life in God's everlasting kingdom. To know that others are on the same road as ourselves is a great comfort. But to have them as companions is better still.

For several years N. and N. were making their separate ways along the path of life. But at a certain point their paths met, and they made the decision to travel the rest of life's journey together.

We are gathered here today to witness them committing themselves to one another and to their common journey. We are in the presence of love, for only love could motivate people to take a step like this. This means we are also in the presence of God, for where love is, God is.

Wedding Ceremony without Mass

Therefore let us pause briefly to draw near to him, and to ask his blessing on all of us, and especially on N. and N. [*Pause*]

Opening Prayer

Let us pray:

Heavenly Father, today N. and N. commit themselves to one another, and set out on the road of married life. May the lamp of love always light their way, so that they will be able to follow their chosen road to the end in freedom, joy and peace. We ask this through Christ our Lord.

Wedding within Mass

Penitential Rite

Let us pause briefly to call to mind God's presence with us now and at every step of life's journey. [*Pause*]
Let us ask his forgiveness for sometimes doubting him.
I confess to almighty God.

Opening Prayer

Cf. Roman Missal

Readings on pages 92.

Homily

Marriage implies the coming together of two people and two lives. However, if a real communion is to take place, this coming together must be not only one of bodies but also one of minds and hearts. "Physical relationship divorced from spiritual is body without soul." (Gandhi).

But this coming together doesn't mean that the two become completely one. They don't fuse in such a way that they become a third person. They are not two streams, once separate, which converge and coalesce. The partners keep their individual identities, and this is a good thing.

Hence, a better example than that of the streams is that of two travellers, travelling on different paths, who meet and decide to travel together from that point on. We are not talking about two strangers who chance to meet when out for an afternoon stroll, and who decide to finish their stroll together. We are talking about a man and woman, on the great and unretraceable path of life, who meet and make the momentous decision that from that point on they will become fellow travellers. They decide to share, not just a few moments or hours of their time, but all the rest of their lives.

"Will you walk the rest of life's road with me? Are you willing to share everything, your whole life, with me as I am with you? Are you prepared to make a total gift of yourself, body, heart, and spirit to me as I am to you?" To give an unqualified "yes" to these questions is a huge undertaking. To commit one's hopes and dreams, one's entire life and destiny to another human being, is an enormous thing to do.

When, as the Bible says, "the two become one", there is a certain loss. There is, for instance, a loss of independence. Each can no longer "go it alone". But there is a far greater gain. A great sharing and enrichment results. For a start, they now have companionship. How swiftly and sweetly the milestones go by when we have pleasant company. They also have mutual support and encouragement so that they are able to take the difficulties in their stride, indeed hardly notice them. But above all they now have a thing called "love", without which we all are forlorn travellers on this earth.

It is interesting to consider how the paths of the partners meet. Sometimes the meeting seems completely accidental. But is anything accidental? Other times it seems as if an invisible friendly hand steered them gently towards one another. Sometimes the decision to travel henceforward together is taken quickly. There is, as it were, instant recognition. He believes in her, and she believes in him. In other cases the decision comes only after their paths have crossed and recrossed many times. During this time trust has been growing, and finally the decision is made.

No matter the circumstances in which their paths meet, the person with faith is able to say: "Here is a companion, given me by God, with whom I can share the rest of my journey." The journey we're talking about is not just any journey. It is that unique and wonderful journey, the journey of life, a journey which, according to faith, is a homeward one to God's eternal kingdom.

Well, N. and N. met, and have decided to travel the rest of the way together. We are here to witness them commit themselves to one another and to this common journey. We pray that God will bless and guide them in their journey, a journey which we hope will be a long and happy one. Above all we pray that he will help them make the journey from selfishness to true love. Whether married or single, this is a journey we all have to make. In a sense, it is the real journey of life.

"Don't walk ahead of me, I may not follow; don't walk behind me, I may not lead; just walk beside me and be my friend." (Albert Camus).

"When friendly paths meet the whole world becomes like home." (Hermann Hesse).

Prayer of the Faithful

President: It is from God that we come when we enter this life, and it is to him we go when we leave it. This means that though we may be travelling along separate paths, we are in fact all going in the same direction. Let us pray to God for the grace to be truly helpful to one another.

Response: Lord, hear our prayer.

Reader(s): For all those who believe in Christ: that they may hear his commandment of love, and obey it. Let us pray to the Lord.

For those who hold public office: that they may judge wisely and act fairly. let us pray to the Lord.

For N. and N.: that their common path may be lit up by the lamp of a true and faithful love for one another. Let us pray to the Lord.

Now that their paths have joined, may no selfishness, pride, or weakness separate them. Let us pray to the Lord.

For all married couples: that they may keep in mind the love which brought them together in the first place, and so continue to offer one another companionship, support, and faithful love. Let us pray to the Lord.

For all those who travel down the road of life alone: that they may find companionship. Let us pray to the Lord.

Let us now pray for our own special intentions. [*Pause*] Let us pray to the Lord.

President: God, our Father, grant us in all our tasks your help, in all our doubts your guidance, in all our weaknesses your strength, in all our sorrows your comfort, and in all our dangers your protection. We ask this through Christ our Lord.

(Communion) Reflection

No. 3 or No. 13.

8. BUILDING A RELATIONSHIP

Introduction

In the name of the Father and of the Son and of the Holy Spirit.
The grace of our Lord Jesus Christ, the love of God, and the fellowship of the Holy Spirit be with you all.

A lone tree on a hilltop is at the mercy of every wind that blows. In the same way a human being who has no ties with others is at the mercy of the cold winds of anguish and loneliness.
We need ties with other human beings. Not just superficial ties, but ties of love and friendship. For our wholeness, for our mental health, each of us needs a friend.
N. and N. have been developing a close friendship for some time. Today they are cementing their friendship. They are committing themselves to one another in marriage. The whole Church is happy for them, and prays that they will find warmth and closeness in their marriage.

Wedding Ceremony without Mass

Though we long for closeness we also fear it, because we know that it makes demands on us. Let us ask God to help us with his grace to live up to the demands of friendship [*Pause*]

Opening Prayer

Let us pray:
God, our Father, your love for us is everlasting. Bless N. and N., who today are being united in marriage. Bind them to one another in a loving and trusting relationship. May they find in this relationship that warmth, tenderness, and human closeness we all need and long for. We ask this through Christ our Lord.

Wedding within Mass

Penitential Rite

Each of us is wounded by sin and selfishness. We fear closeness with others because it makes demands on us. Let us reflect on our sinfulness and need of God's help. *[Pause]*

Christ did not hesitate to get close to us. In fact he became a brother to us. Let us ask his help and forgiveness.

Lord, you reveal to us the mystery of the Father's presence among us and love for us. Lord, have mercy.

You remind us of our dignity as his sons and daughters, and you help us to live up to this dignity. Christ, have mercy.

You are by our side when we have to walk through the valley of darkness to give us courage, strength, and hope. Lord, have mercy

Opening Prayer

Cf. Roman Missal

Readings on page 93.

Homily

In his book, *The Little Prince*, Antoine de Saint Exupery tells the story of a small boy who came to earth from another planet. On earth he felt very lonely and longed for a friend. One day he met a fox who was as desperate for friendship as he was. He asked the fox to play with him.

"I can't because no one has taken the trouble to tame me," the fox answered.

"What does 'to tame' mean?" asked the Little Prince

"It means to establish ties," the fox replied.

"And what does 'to establish ties' mean?" the Little Prince persisted.

"Just that," said the fox. "To me you are still nothing more than a little boy like a thousand other little boys. And to you I am nothing more than a fox like a thousand other foxes. But if you tame me, then to me you will be unique in all the world. And to you I will be unique in all the world."

"I'm beginning to understand," said the Little Prince.

"My life is very monotonous," the fox went on. "I hunt chickens; people hunt me. But if you tame me, it will be as if the sun came to shine on my life. I shall know the sound of a step that will be different from all other steps. Other steps send me hurrying back underground. Yours will call me, like music, out of my burrow. Please tame me."

"I'd like to," said the Little Prince, "but I don't have much time. I have a great many things to understand."

"One understands only the things that one tames," said the fox. "People have no more time to understand anything. They buy things all ready-made at the shops. But there is no shop anywhere where one can buy friendship, and so people have no friends any more. If you want a friend, tame me."

"What must I do to tame you?" asked the Little Prince.

"You must be very patient," replied the fox. "First you will sit down a little distance from me in the grass. I shall look at you out of the corner of my eye, and you will say nothing. Words are a source of misunderstanding. But you will sit a little closer to me every day."

The Little Prince agreed, and so it was that he tamed the fox and they became the best of friends.

We all long for friendship. We pine for closeness and love. Yet while we desire these things we also fear them. Why is this? A close relationship makes demands on us. We cannot have closeness unless we are prepared to love. But when we love we become vulnerable. We can be hurt if the other person does not respond in kind. For this reason many settle for shallow and transient attachments rather than for close and permanent relationships.

Wherever you find a good marriage you will find a deep relationship. But depth is the thing which is most lacking in relationships between men and women today. A deep relationship does not just happen. It has to be built. The building of it takes time and effort. Haste ruins everything. It is useless to plant an acorn today and expect to sit in the shade of an oak tree tomorrow.

In building a relationship small things are very important. We have to try to achieve intimacy in the little things of every day. We have to notice, see, and take an interest in one another.

One of the most necessary things in any relationship is trust. This is especially true of a marriage relationship. In marriage we do not just trust another person with one thing and for one occasion, but with everything and forever. Trust must be cultivated. It is built on discipline, reliability, and constancy. When trust is betrayed great hurt results, and the relationship begins to crumble.

We pray that N. and N. will take the time and make the effort to build up a really good relationship in which they will find closeness, intimacy and love. May they truly tame one another and, like the fox and the Little Prince, become the best of friends.

"It is useless to seek happiness elsewhere than in human relationships." (Antoine de Saint Exupery).

"I pine for one to whom I can speak my first thoughts. I know no one to whom I can be transparent instinctively." (Thoreau).

Prayer of the Faithful

President: It was not we who first loved God. It was God who first loved us, and sent his Son to us to be the expiation of our sins. Let us ask him to touch our hearts, and make us people who are capable of love and friendship.

Response: Lord, hear our prayer.

Reader(s): For the Church: that its leaders may build it into a true community, where people can find warmth and closeness. Let us pray to the Lord.

For those who hold public office: that their deeds may match their words and promises. Let us pray to the Lord.

For N. and N.: that they may build a relationship in which they will find that intimacy and tenderness we all need and secretly long for. Let us pray to the Lord.

That they may not be afraid of trials and difficulties, because there is more depth in a relationship which has weathered storms. Let us pray to the Lord.

For all married couples: that the partners may strive to be true and loyal friends to one another. Let us pray to the Lord.

For all those who are lonely, and who long for love and friendship. Let us pray to the Lord.

For our personal needs which we now bring before God in silence. *[Pause]* Let us pray to the Lord.

President: Heavenly Father, help us to be conscious of the fact that the quality of our presence, looks, words, and deeds brings happiness or misery, life or death to those with whom we live; and realising this may we strive always to treat them the way we would like them to treat us. We ask this through Christ our Lord.

(Communion) Reflection

No. 8 or No. 9.

9. BUILDING ON ROCK

Introduction

In the name of the Father and of the Son and of the Holy Spirit.
The grace and peace of God our Father and the Lord Jesus Christ be with you.

Today N. and N. are setting out to build a very important house — the house of their marriage. People enter marriage with great hopes and dreams. But many place their hopes on flimsy things and build on weak foundations.

The teaching of Christ shows us the way to go. To those who listen to his words and who act on them, he makes a wonderful promise. He says they are building the house of their lives on solid rock.

Wedding Ceremony without Mass

Let us pause for a moment of reflection. Let us seek Christ's help and guidance for ourselves, and especially for N. and N. on this great day for them. [*Pause*]

Opening Prayer

Let us pray:
Father, your love for us in the same yesterday, today, and forever. Bless N. and N., who today are being united in the sacrament of marriage. May the house of their marriage be built not only on physical fidelity but also fidelity of the heart. Thus they will be able to live in love and harmony with one another, and in peace with others. We make this prayer through Christ our Lord.

Wedding within Mass

Penitential Rite

Let us pause for a moment to look into our lives to see what place, what importance, we give to the teachings of Christ. [*Pause*]

Let us now turn to him in confidence, and ask him for help and guidance.

Lord, you help us to place our trust in God rather than in money. Lord, have mercy.

You help us to realise that it is more blessed to give than to receive. Christ, have mercy.

You help us to realise that to live rightly is what life is about. Lord, have mercy.

Opening Prayer

Cf. Roman Missal

Readings on page 97.

Homily

The most important part of a house is largely invisible, so much so that normally we don't even think about it. But a builder does. In fact it the very first thing he thinks about. I'm talking about the foundation.

The foundation has to be deep and solid. In a word — rocklike. To put down such a foundation calls for careful planning, time, and a lot of hard, unspectacular work. Months go by and there is still nothing to be seen above ground. To the uninitiated time is being wasted.

But the wise builder knows differently. He takes his time. He will not be rushed. He is thinking far into the future. In his mind's eye he already sees the completed building. He sees people living in it, people who have invested their all in that house. He sees the house being beaten by rain and lashed by wind. He knows that the fate of that house and its occupants will depend on the soundness of the foundation he is now laying down.

The foolish builder, on the other hand, is in a hurry. He can't be bothered to go down deep, and he is not too concerned about the quality of the materials he uses. He doesn't hesitate to cut corners. He is not looking to the future. He does not allow himself to think about the people who will live in the house, or the storms that will inevitably assail it. His only concern is to get it up as quickly and as cheaply as possible.

Building a marriage could be compared to building a house. Like a house it does not appear overnight. You do not take possession of the house of marriage all ready-made on your wedding day. It has to be built. In building it, it is essential that we look to the future because this house has to last, not just for a few years, but for the rest of our lives. And we can be sure that some gales will be let loose upon it. Hence the importance of laying down a good foundation. We have to build not on sand but on rock. What are the "rocks" on which we should build the house of our marriage. Here are a few of them.

Fidelity: This is not just another rock. It is a precious stone, a true gem. We're not talking only about physical fidelity, but also fidelity of the heart.

Trust: Without mutual trust the marriage relationship won't even get off the ground. Trust is the most precious thing I can give to another person. As for receiving it — I must not think that I deserve it by right. I must so act as to make myself worthy of it.

Gentleness: To many gentleness means weakness. Nothing could be further from the truth. Gentleness is not a form of weakness. It is a form of great strength. It takes a strong, self-confident person to be gentle. It is one of the most necessary things, not just in marriage, but in life in general.

Communication: Unless we are able to communicate we are not better than stones. Even though we may be physically close, nothing passes between us. But when we are able to communicate well and deeply, then life flows from one to the other.

Acceptance: Acceptance of each other's individuality is the only foundation on which to build a mature marriage, one on which real love can grow.

Faith in God: By ourselves we are very limited. We are weakened by sin and tainted with selfishness. We are incapable of unselfish love and rocklike constancy. Hence we need the help only God can give.

Love: This is the mortar which binds all these stones together. There are many words to express love. This is good, because it takes many shapes and forms. However, we are not really talking about words. To build on words, no matter how fine they might be, is, as Christ said, to build on sand. We are talking about a love which is expressed in deeds.

What N. and N. are called to build is not a building of stones and mortar, but a tiny human community, one in which they will be able to find warmth, acceptance, a sense of belonging, and peace. Without these, even though they may be living in a mansion, they won't find in it what they are looking for.

We pray that the house of their marriage will, with the Lord's help, endure. We pray also that they will find in it what their hearts are longing for.

"Trust is the sun that should rise with us each morning and go to sleep with us each night." (Catherine de Hueck Doherty).

"What good is there in a love that must be watched all the time?" (Dostoyevsky).

Prayer of the Faithful

President: Let us pray for the wisdom, courage, and strength to be able to build our lives, not on the values of the world, but on those of the Gospel.

Response: Lord, hear us in your love.

Reader(s): For all the followers of Christ: that they may not love merely in word or speech but in deed and truth. Let us pray in faith.

For all our political and civil leaders: that their deeds may match their words and promises. Let us pray in faith.

For N. and N.: that their love for each other may be so true and solid that the house of their marriage will stand firm for the whole of their lives. Let us pray in faith.

That they may not be afraid of the inevitable storms which will assail this fragile house, but be confident that they can withstand these with faith in Christ and in one another. Let us pray in faith.

For all here present: that we may derive joy and hope for our lives from this celebration. Let us pray in faith.

For those who cannot see beyond the values of this world, and who pin their hopes on things that are flimsy and unreliable. Let us pray in faith.

Now let us pray in our own special needs and intentions. [*Pause*] Let us pray in faith.

President: Heavenly Father, grant us in all our tasks your help, in all our doubts your guidance, in all our weaknesses your strength, in all our sorrows your consolation, and in all our dangers your protection. We ask this through Christ our Lord.

(Communion) Reflection

No. 5 or No. 3.

10. THE BOND OF LOVE

Introduction

In the name of the Father and of the Son and of the Holy Spirit.
The Lord be with you.

As yet the lives of N. and N. are their own. Their destinies are still separate. But after today all this will have changed. Their lives will be linked together. Their destinies will be inextricably bound up with one another.

During this ceremony they will bind themselves to one another by a very special bond — the bond of marriage. God blesses this bond and wishes it to endure.

Wedding Ceremony without Mass

Unfortunately, even after the most solemn promises, through human weakness and selfishness, we may still be tempted to forget our commitments and go our separate ways. Let us therefore ask God to help us, and especially N. and N., to be true to our promises and faithful to one another. [*Pause*]

Opening Prayer

Let us pray:

Heavenly Father, hear our prayers for N. and N. Bless the covenant of love they are entering today. Seal the bond of marriage by which they will be no longer two but one in mind and heart. Bind them closely to you and to one another. We do not ask that this bond will never be tested, but only that it will be strong enough to endure whatever comes. We make this prayer through Christ our Lord.

Wedding within Mass

Penitential Rite

The Eucharist, which we are about to celebrate, creates a bond between the disciples of Christ, a bond which he wishes to endure so that they may produce in the world the fruits of love.

Let us pause to call to mind our sins which weaken our ties with Christ and with our brothers and sisters. [*Pause*]

Lord, you are the vine, we are the branches. Lord, have mercy.

Separated from you and from one another, our lives become barren. Christ, have mercy.

United with you and with one another, our lives become fruitful. Lord, have mercy.

Opening Prayer

Cf. Roman Missal

Readings on page 99.

Homily

When two climbers set out to conquer a difficult mountain peak they link themselves to one another by means of a rope. So, from that point on, their fates are inextricably intertwined with one another. They are more interdependent than two leaves on the same branch.

The decision to link themselves together calls for an enormous amount of mutual trust. To make it work calls for a enormous amount of cooperation. If each plays his (her) part, and if they pull together, they have an excellent chance of making it to the top. But if one opts out, or if they pull against one another, they both risk falling into the abyss.

To link their lives together imposes considerable restraints and disciplines on them. They also lose something — a certain amount of personal freedom is surrendered. One cannot make a major move without consulting the other. But of course they gain a lot more than they lose. They now have mutual support and enjoy a certain security. They no longer have to rely solely on their own strength. Two pulling together can do what one cannot.

Why do they do this? They do so because they have a common goal which they wish to attain, namely, to reach the top of the mountain. They have no wish to make prisoners out of one another. Rather they wish to pull one another upwards.

When two people get married we talk about them "tying the knot". Thus we acknowledge that a bond is formed between them. Like it or not, from this day forward their lives are linked together. Their destinies are inextricably bound up with one another. In a word, they are like climbers on the one rope.

They know that when they decide to enter into this bond they lose something. A certain amount of personal independence is lost. But they are convinced that they stand to gain a lot more. The bond is not a fetter, not a chain which makes one or both feel like a prisoner. Rather it is a lifeline which provides them with companionship, friendship, and mutual support.

To link one's entire future, one's whole life, to that of another person is an enormous thing to do. It implies a huge amount of faith in that person. Hence it is not something which can be undertaken lightly. The partners must not only know what they are doing but also know each other. And it must be done in complete freedom. It is *they* who are tying the knot. It is not the Church or the State. They are not being driven into this union. They are being drawn into it by their love for one another. Without love the bond of marriage would quickly become a fetter.

Today N. and N. are joining their lives in this public ceremony. They are binding themselves to one another. The bond with which they do so is not made of some unbreakable material. We can be sure, too, that it will be tested by life. It will be subjected to God alone knows what stresses and strains.

It will also be subjected to what you might call the normal wear and tear of human relationships. However, each partner is determined to play his (her) part, and is hoping that the other will do likewise. No one wants to tie one's life to a frail thread and live in daily expectation of seeing it snap, or to discover that it has not, after all, been fastened to anything solid.

What is it that weakens and endangers this bond? Lack of trust, lack of real communication, and selfishness — these knaw away at it. But infidelity hacks at it with a knife. What strengthens the bond? Trust, good communication, mutual thoughtfulness, and of course fidelity, not just physical fidelity, but fidelity of the heart. These reinforce and seal the bond.

In and through his Son Jesus, God the Father has bound himself to each of us and to the entire human family in a covenant of love which can never be broken. He is happy to see N. and N. binding themselves to one another in love. He blesses the bond which they are forming with one another today. This sacred knot on which so much depends, and on which God, through the ministry of the Church, puts his seal, must not be broken. With the help of his grace it will not be broken.

"If there was no risk, there would be no love." (Michel Quoist).

"If I insist on giving only to myself, I shall receive nothing." (Antoine de Saint Exupery).

Prayer of the Faithful

President: In and through his Son, God the Father has bound himself to us in an everlasting covenant of love. Let us pray to him, asking him to strengthen the bonds that bind us to him and to one another.

Response: Lord, hear us in your love.

Reader(s): For the Christian community: that it may be a sign of unity and an instrument of peace in a divided world. We pray in faith.

For world leaders: that they may take the path of reconciliation and peace rather than that of confrontation and war. We pray in faith.

For N. and N.: that the frail human bond which joins their lives today may never be broken. We pray in faith.

That this bond may bind them together in a union, not only of body, but also of mind and heart. We pray in faith.

For people whose marriages are under stress: that they may have the courage to seek help in their difficulties. We pray in faith.

For marriages that have broken down: that Christ may heal the wounds that result. We pray in faith.

For single and widowed people: that they may find love and support in the Christian community. We pray in faith.

President: Merciful Father, fill our hearts with your love. Give us the grace to rise above our human weakness, and keep us faithful to you and to one another. We ask this through Christ our Lord.

(Communion) Reflection

No 10 or No. 9.

11. IT'S NOT GOOD TO BE ALONE

Introduction

In the name of the Father and of the Son and of the Holy Spirit.
The grace of our Lord Jesus Christ, the love of God, and the fellowship of the Holy Spirit be with you all.

No human being is an island, complete in itself. Each of us forms part of the continent of humanity. Hence it is not good for us to be alone. We need the company, support, and love of other human beings.

Here is where marriage comes in. The Bible teaches that marriage comes from God. Through marriage a man and a woman can achieve that closeness we all need and pine for.

We can be confident then that God is with us today as we gather to witness N. and N. commit themselves to one another in the sacrament of marriage.

Wedding Ceremony without Mass

Let us reflect for a moment on God's love for us, and ask his blessing on N. and N., and on all gathered here. [*Pause*]

Opening Prayer

Let us pray:
God, our Father, we are your children. You put us on this earth not to live alone but in community with others, sharing one another's joys, and bearing one another's burdens. Hear our prayers for N. and N., who today are joining their lives in marriage. Casting aside all doubts and fears, may they open their hearts fully, and give themselves unreservedly, to one another. Thus they will build a community of love and peace. We make this prayer through Christ our Lord.

Wedding within Mass

Penitential Rite

Let us reflect for a moment on our lives to see how we sometimes use other people. We take from them but are not always willing to give to them. [*Pause*]

God is the one who never abandons us but always gives us the support of his presence.

Lord, you are faithful in all your words and loving in all your deeds. Lord, have mercy.

You support all who fall, and raise up all who are bowed down. Christ, have mercy.

You are close to all who call on you, who call on you from their hearts. Lord, have mercy.

Opening Prayer

Cf. Roman Missal

Readings on page 102.

Homily

To plant a tree by itself on a hilltop is not to give it a fair chance. To do so is to expose it to every wind that blows, with the result that it will be a poor, stunted specimen, a mere shadow of what it could be. If you want a tree to grow to its full potential you must plant it in a more sheltered spot. Ideally you should also plant at least one other tree by its side. The trees should be more or less equal.

They must not be planted so close together that they smother one another, or become so intertwined that if one is removed, the other falls down. Yet they must not be so far apart that they are unable to give anything to one another. They must be so planted as to be able to give shelter and shade to one another, without in any way hindering one another's growth.

The Bible says, "It is not good for man to be alone." This means that God made us for community, not for a solitary life. We need other people in order to become all that God intended us to become. Without a close relationship with at least one other human being we will be at the mercy of the cold winds of anguish and loneliness, and will suffer as a result.

It was for this reason, as well as for the growth of the human family, that God make the first man a "helpmate". And so, leaving his parents, the man joined himself to this helpmate, and they became "one body". To be one body is to be covenanted together, each in need of the other, each having a special gift to give the other, so that they complement each other.

After marriage the partners are a little like two trees planted side by side. They must be sufficiently close to one another as to be able to provide mutual support. Yet they must not be so close as to stifle one another. Their lives must not become so intertwined that they lose their individuality. They must preserve their identities. Each must allow the other the space and freedom to grow.

This demands a special kind of love. False love seeks to keep the other in subjection. It dreads the idea that the other should have a separate life — thoughts, interests, career, friends, even goals of his (her) own. True love, on the other hand, respects the right, indeed the need, of the other to be a n autonomous person. It gives the other room to grow in his (her) own inimitable way. To let someone we love go entirely free and live his (her) own life, is the most difficult thing in the world.

Hence, while closeness is necessary and highly desirable in a relationship such as marriage, there must be spaces too, if each partner is to develop to his (her) full potential. The real challenge is this: how to be together, close, even intimate with one another, without smothering or dominating one another. To smother would be to deny all that is best in the other. To dominate would be to suppress it.

The couple must be united by such a love for one another that their separateness and loneliness are overcome, yet they are free to be themselves. Their differences are not denied, much less suppressed. Rather they are encouraged, and so become a source of mutual enrichment. It is because you are different from me that you have something to give me. If you are just a mirror-image of me, then I have no need of you.

Today N. and N. are offering themselves to one another in marriage. They are in effect saying to each other: "I am ready to stand by your side. I'll be there with you, yet I have no desire to smother, dominate, or possess you. I'll be there to help you to grow to your full potential. I hope that you can do the same for me."

Two trees cannot receive everything they need from one another. They must also receive from outside sources — from the sun, the rain, the soil, and so on. In the same way a couple cannot give to one another all that they need. They must be open to receive from outside sources — from others and, above all, from God our heavenly Father. After all, we are not trees. We are his precious children. He wants to see us grow and have life.

"Differences are not a threat but a treasure." (Jean Vanier).

"I have nothing to give another person; but I have a duty to open him to his own life, to allow him to be himself." (Michel Quoist).

Prayer of the Faithful

President: Let us pray to God that he may take away our hearts of stone and give us hearts that are warm and capable of love.

Response: Lord, hear us in your love.

Reader(s): For the Christian community: that its members may truly love and support one another as Christ wished and prayed. Let us pray in faith.

For the heads of governments: that through goodwill and cooperation they may free the world of poverty and oppression, so that all of God's children may live in freedom and dignity. Let us pray in faith.

For N and N.: that their relationship may provide them with love and mutual support, without in any way hindering their individual growth and development. Let us pray in faith.

May they always enjoy the support of good friends, and be open to the help God, and God alone, can give. Let us pray in faith.

For those who are sick, or lonely, or discouraged: that they may draw strength from faith in God and the love of their friends. Let us pray in faith.

For our own personal needs which we now bring before God in silence. [*Pause*] Let us pray in faith.

President: Heavenly Father, fill our hearts with your love. Give us the grace to rise above our human weakness, and keep us faithful to you and to one another. We ask this through Christ our Lord.

(Communion) Reflection

No. 13 or No. 8.

12. WEEDS AMONG THE WHEAT

Introduction

In the name of the Father and of the Son and of the Holy Spirit.

The grace and peace of God our Father and the Lord Jesus Christ be with you.

The world is like a field in which wheat and weeds grow side by side. In others words, it is a mixture of good and evil.

The human heart — that most precious part of each of us — is also divided. It contains a mixture of good and evil, love and hate, light and darkness.

Hence there is no such thing as a marriage between two perfect human beings. Each of us is wounded by sin. We have to accept this reality. N. and N. hopefully have already done so.

Wedding Ceremony without Mass

However, let us reflect on it with them for a moment. [*Pause*] The Lord in whom there is no trace of evil, will help us to overcome the evil which threatens us from inside and outside. Let us turn to him now with confidence.

Opening Prayer

Let us pray:

Father of mercy, we are your children. When we love one another unselfishly we grow like corn in the sun. Hear our prayers for N. and N., who today are pledging their love in the sacrament of marriage. Grant that neither their own selfishness, nor the cynicism of the world, may choke the tender shoots of their love. Through mutual fidelity may they reap a plentiful harvest of joy and peace in their married life. We make this prayer through Christ our Lord.

Wedding within Mass

Penitential Rite

The Lord is the only one is whom there is no shadow or trace of evil.
Let us acknowledge the evil for which we personally are responsible, and
ask his help to overcome it. *[Pause]*

In a world in which indifference to others is rampant, you help us to
be caring people. Lord, have mercy.

In a world filled with greed for material things, you help us to value
and seek the things of the spirit. Christ, have mercy.

In a world filled with selfishness, you help us to be unselfish in our
love. Lord, have mercy.

Opening Prayer

Cf. Roman Missal

Readings on page 104.

Homily

The farmer sowed good seed in his field and than sat back in expectation of a bumper harvest. Soon it looked as if his expectations were
going to be fulfilled. A host of sturdy green shoots sprang up. It brought
joy to his heart to see them sway in the wind and dance in the sun.

However, one morning as he cast his eyes over the field he got a
terrible shock. He saw weeds among the young corn. It wouldn't have
been so bad if there were only a few weeds here and there, but they seemed
to be everywhere. He was desperately disappointed. It came as a terrible
blow. When he looked at the field now, all he could see were the weeds.
The wheat seemed to have become invisible.

So what did he do? At first he wanted to rush out and pull up the weeds.
However, he quickly realised that this was not on. In doing so he would
pull up some of the wheat too. Then he was sorely tempted to plough the
whole field up and start all over again, perhaps with a different field,
except that it was too late in the season.

Eventually he calmed down and was able to see things in better
perspective. What if there were some weeds in his precious field! There

was wheat there too, wheat that was just as green and vibrant as ever. He would have to be humble and patient. He would have to work hard and do everything in his power to encourage the wheat in the hope that it would outgrow the weeds.

And that's exactly what he did. One day he made a discovery which gave him great heart. He noticed that because of the presence of the weeds the wheat was forced to reach and strain upwards. In so doing it grew all the better. When the harvest day came, and he finally separated the wheat from the weeds, to his surprise and delight a fine harvest resulted. Though it fell short of the hundred per cent he had originally hoped for, the quality was excellent , and the quantity was more than enough to meet all his needs. And for some strange reason he got more joy out of reaping this harvest than out of any other.

Something similar happens in every marriage. The partners set out with sky-high expectations. They expect their partner to provide them with continuous friendship and unwavering love. For a while it seems as if their expectations are going to be fulfilled. Living together brings great joy. Each regards the other as a saint.

But time passes and inevitably the weeds appear. To their horror they discover that their partner is riddled with faults and more like a devil than a saint. This causes not just disappointment but hurt as well. They feel let down. "He (she) is not the person I married," is a common lament. Ah, how they would love to pull up those weeds! Not doubt they will try, and when they don't succeed, they may be tempted to look for another partner.

But, hopefully, wisdom will prevail. They will realise that only God is perfect. Only he can love unfailingly. They will come to accept that their partner is neither a saint nor a devil, but a human being and, as such, a mixture of good and evil. When one is conscious of the weeds in one's own field, it becomes easier to accept those in the partner's field. The main thing is not to let the faults blind us to the good that is there too. That would be a tragedy.

The fact is that when two people such as N. and N. get married they bring to each other their riches and poverty, strengths and weaknesses, loves and hates, hurts and wounds. The sooner they accept this situation the better. However, it takes time to get to know the other person's wounds, weaknesses, needs, longings, and good points. It calls for sensitivity, and means spending time together. But the real challenge comes in accepting the other as he (she) is — warts and all, as they say. You never improve people by rejecting them. It is only when we are accepted and loved as we are at present that we are able to change.

The road from selfishness to love is a long and difficult one. It begins by getting to know and accept each other as we are. It is a struggle, but it is precisely through this kind of struggle — the struggle to love an imperfect human being — that we grow.

We must look to God, our heavenly Father, for help and inspiration. He loves us as we are. If we are conscious of being loved unconditionally by him, it will spur us to love our partner, and others, in the same way.

This is our hope and prayer for our friends, N. and N.

"We must accept or refuse one another as we are. I cannot hew the smallest chip out of the character of my friend, either to beautify or deform it." (Thoreau).

"Loving someone is loving him as he is, with all his strengths and weaknesses." (Michel Quoist).

Prayer of the Faithful

President: Confident that good is stronger than evil, and that love is more powerful than hate, let us turn to the Lord of the harvest for the help we need to overcome evil and do good.

Response: Lord, graciously hear us.

Reader(s): For the Church: that it may always be a place in which both sinners and saints can feel at home. Lord, hear us.

For the world in which we live: that in spite of all the obstacles and difficulties, the human family may grow in understanding and cooperation. Lord, hear us.

For N. and N.: that the faults they find in one another may never blind them to the good that is there too; that they may love and accept one another as they are. Lord, hear us.

That they may rejoice with one another in moments of strength, and be compassionate towards one another in moments of weakness. Lord, hear us.

For all those who have been hurt and wounded by the attitude of other people: that they may find acceptance and healing. Lord, hear us.

That each of us, while acknowledging our weakness and sinfulness, may realise that the greatest thing about us is our capacity for goodness. Lord, hear us.

Let us now pray to God for our own special needs. [*Pause*] Lord, hear us.

President: Heavenly Father, we are like seeds planted by you in the same field. Together we sway in the wind; together we soak in the sun. Grant that we may never hinder one another's growth. Rather, may we help one another to grow to our full potential. We ask this through Christ our Lord.

(Communion) Reflection

No. 6 or No. 12.

13. FOUR REQUIREMENTS

Introduction

In the name of the Father and of the Son and of the Holy Spirit.

The grace of our Lord Jesus Christ, the love of God, and the fellowship of the Holy Spirit be with you all.

The Bible says that when God made us, he made us in his own image and likeness. This is the greatest statement ever made about human dignity. We are most like God, we best live up to our dignity, when we are truly loving people.

N. and N. are about to get married. Nothing provides a greater challenge to love, or offers such opportunities for its practice, as marriage. Marriage is rooted and grounded in love. A marriage without love is like a flower garden without flowers.

But true and genuine love does not come easy to us. By nature we all are selfish. We tend to put ourselves first. Hence we need the Holy Spirit to touch our hearts so that we can love unselfishly.

Wedding Ceremony without Mass

Let us be silent for a moment to call down the blessing, help, and guidance of God's Spirit on N. and N., and on all here present. [*Pause*]

Opening Prayer

Let us pray:

Father, look with love on N. and N., who are about to enter the state of marriage. Help them to stand by one another in good times and in bad. May their love prove itself by the sacrifices they make for one another. May they discover that there is more joy in giving than in receiving. Write their names on the palm of your hand, and keep them faithful forever. We ask this through Christ our Lord.

Wedding within Mass

Penitential Rite

Let us reflect for a moment on the fact that our love blows hot and cold and, even at best, is riddled with imperfections. [*Pause*]

Now let us confess our sins to God, especially our lack of love, confident that he is generous with his forgiveness.

I confess to almighty God.

Opening Prayer

Cf. Roman Missal

Readings on page 107.

Homily

In the early stages of World War I, a Russian officer and his regiment were left behind in enemy territory. All the generals had retreated hack into Russia to regroup and reorganise. The officer's first thought was to save himself and his men. It would not be difficult because the border was within easy reach.

But he realised that someone had to remain. There was a huge gap through which the enemy would pour. Whole regiments would be cut to pieces as they retreated in disorder. This gap had to be plugged for at least a long as it took to get the wounded over the border. If he didn't attempt to do it no one else would. There simply was no one else around.

He lined up his men in ranks. As he looked at their tired faces he felt for them, and wondered what approach he should use in asking them to stay behind and make a stand. After deep consideration he saw four essential needs.

1. He first of all decided that he would tell them exactly what was involved. He felt it would be wrong to deceive them. So he told them the magnitude of the task facing them, and the dangers inherent in it.

2. He decided not to command them even though as their officer he was fully entitled to do so. He told them that he wanted only volunteers. What he was asking was so enormous that it seemed only right they

should have a choice in the matter. Besides, it's no good forcing people to make sacrifices.

3. He impressed on them that once they had decided to stay behind, there could be no going back on that decision. Once they had committed themselves they would no longer be free to run away when the going got rough. To do so would be to make the lot of their comrades all the more perilous. Their only hope of survival lay in sticking together.

4. How could he motivate them? To what could he appeal in asking such a sacrifice from them? He could promise them no rewards, not even survival. He decided to resort to love. Only love could make this kind of sacrifice possible, and perhaps even sweeten it. He asked them to do it for the sake of their fellow soldiers in the rest of the army, to save them from being cut to pieces.

When he had put these four things to them, he asked those who wanted to volunteer to take one step forward. Every single one of his men stepped forward.

N. and N. are about to get married. The decision to get married may not be quite as momentous as that which faced these soldiers. Nevertheless, it is a very big decision. It affects the whole future of N. and N., and indeed the future of others too. It is not, then, a step that can be taken lightly, which is why the Church requires certain things of people entering marriage. These come down pretty well to the same four things the officer demanded of his men.

1. It requires that they know what it is they are committing themselves to. No one should walk into a marriage with eyes closed.

2. It requires that they freely consent to this step. Any kind of coercion would render their consent null and void.

3. It requires that once the step is taken there must be no going back. Marriage is a lifelong commitment. There can be no running out when difficulties occur; otherwise a lot of hurt will result. From this day forward the partners carry each other's hopes and dreams in their hands.

4. In asking for a decision which involves all this, to what does the Church appeal? To love. The decision to get married should be based, not on the hope of material gain or anything like that, but on mutual love. A marriage without love is like a fireplace without a fire.

Of the four requirements, love is the most important. What kind of love are we talking about? That very practical, down-to-earth kind we heard St Paul talk about in the second reading. A love like that does not come easy. It has to be learnt. To enter marriage is to enter a school of love, a school in which all of us are slow learners.

Let N. and N. not be afraid to turn to God for help. He is close to them as they make this great decision. And even though the future is shrouded in uncertainty, they can go forward in hope, trusting in him and in each other. Adventurers are not afraid of uncertainty. They thrive on it. Love is the greatest adventure of all.

"To love blindly is to love selfishly." (Thomas Merton).

"Mankind would perish if there were no exhibition any time and anywhere of the divine in man." (Ghandi).

Prayer of the Faithful

President: St Paul says that without love we are nothing at all. This is true not just for Christians but for all human beings. Without love we are a lamp that does not give light. But when we do love we are at our brightest and best. Let us pray then to our heavenly Father for the grace to be able to love.

Response: Lord, hear our prayer.

Reader(s): For the Church: that its leaders may guide it in a spirit of love and right judgement. Let us pray to the Lord.

For all government leaders: that they may work unselfishly for the good of all their people, but especially of the poorer and weaker members of society. Let us pray to the Lord.

For N. and N.: that God may bless the bond with which they have linked their lives today, and through his grace make it truly unbreakable. Let us pray to the Lord.

That each may find in the other a true and faithful friend. Let us pray to the Lord.

For all here present: that no matter what our state in life, we may be people who are capable of a true and faithful love of others. Let us pray to the Lord.

Let us now bring before God our personal needs, worries, and problems. [*Pause*] Let us pray to the Lord.

President: Heavenly Father, you are the same yesterday, today, and
forever. Help us to have confidence in your unchanging love
for us, so that when things are difficult we may persevere in
goodness and faithfulness. We ask this through Christ our
Lord.

(Communion) Reflection

No.10 or No.11.

14. CROSSING THE BRIDGE

Introduction

In the name of the Father and of the Son and of the Holy Spirit.
The grace and peace of God the Father and the Lord Jesus Christ be with you.

N. and N. are about to take the most important step of their lives, a step which is irreversible. Right now they are single. They are standing as it were on one side of a great bridge. In a little while they will exchange their wedding vows. In doing so they will cross over this bridge and enter a new land — the land of married life. We have come here to encourage them, to wish them well, and to pray for them.

The decision to marry someone is a huge commitment to make to that person. Of course there is doubt. Of course there is uncertainty. Of course there is risk, But where there is also mutual love and trust, these will gradually disappear.

God is with us at all times. But he is especially close to us at the great moments of decision-making in our lives.

Wedding Ceremony without Mass

Let us pause briefly to bring our doubts and fears into his presence, and to seek his help and guidance. [*Pause*]

Opening Prayer

Let us pray:
Father of mercy and love, hear our prayers for N. and N., who are about to pledge their love to one another in the sacrament of marriage. May the Holy Spirit instil in them a deep trust in you and in one another. Thus may they be able to face the future confident that nothing in this life will part them. We make this prayer through Christ our Lord.

Wedding within Mass

Penitential Rite

Now let us ask God's forgiveness for our sins so that we can go forward more freely. [*Pause*]
I confess to almighty God.

Opening Prayer

Cf. Roman Missal

Readings on page 109.

Homily

Imagine for a moment that you are crossing a bridge and have reached the mid-point. You have crossed lots of bridges in your time. However, this one is different. Once you cross it you can never come back. The importance of the step you are about to take suddenly hits you and stops you in your tracks. You cannot just walk casually across. There is too much at stake. Your whole future hangs on this step. You have to do some serious thinking. You feel very lonely, for decision-making is a lonely business.

The first thing you do is look back. You quickly survey the things that are back there and which you are about to surrender. How they line up and present themselves to you one by one! Now that you are about to say goodbye to them in a farewell that is as final as death, they assume an exaggerated importance — yes, all those things which you have so often taken for granted. We are not talking merely about material things.

Then you look ahead of you, and start to think of what you are hoping to find on the other side — the things which motivated you to cross the bridge in the first place. Without doubt, at least from here, they appear very attractive. Still, they are not yet yours. They are in the future. So, for a while at least, you will have to live on hope, which means there is risk and uncertainty.

But suddenly a new thought occurs to you. So far you have been considering only what you are leaving behind you and what you are hoping to find up ahead. But now you begin to think of the most important thing of all, namely, what you are taking with you. Once again we are not talking about material possessions, but about something far more precious. What is it that you take with you?

Basically yourself, that is, the kind of person you are, or what you have made of yourself. This is the only thing that is truly yours. No one can take it from you, though you can agree to share it.

Lo! What is this? Suddenly there is someone at your side, someone who is saying goodbye to precious things too, and all because of a commitment to you. Someone who like you is uncertain about the future, but who is willing to walk into that future with you. Someone, moreover, who is ready to share everything with you, yes, including herself. Suddenly you're no longer lonely and indecisive. So, you join hands, and with your eyes fixed only on the next step ahead, you begin to cross over together, encouraged by the prayers and good wishes of your relatives and friends, who have come to this point with you.

Getting married could be compared to crossing a bridge. The couple leave one world and enter another. There are things they have to give up. Basically what they give up is the single way of life and all it entails. So there is a loss. But there are things they hope to gain — much more than they are losing. Basically what they hope to gain is a life of love and union. However, they cannot gain the good things of the new world unless they are prepared to let go of those of the old world.

N. and N. are now standing at the mid-point of the bridge. They are about to pass the point of no return. They do not take this step lightly. They have thought hard about it and prepared diligently for it. It is a decisive moment for them. Their whole future hangs on it. But it is moments such as this — moments of decision-making, challenge, sacrifice, and risk— which help us to grow.

Hand in hand, they are about to walk into the future. That future will no doubt bring satisfactions and disappointments, successes and failures, pleasures and pain, joys and sorrows. We know that these things come in varying measures to every life.

We are with them. Our prayers and good wishes will put wind in their sails. And of course God is with them. He was with them before. He is with them now, and he awaits them on the other side. Let them go forward then in faith, hope and love.

"The heart of one person holds inexhaustible sources of life for the heart of another." (Dostoyevsky).

"Do not condemn us to be alone when together. Allow us to be together when alone." (Helder Camara).

Prayer of the Faithful

President: At the Last Supper Jesus prayed to his heavenly Father for the gift of unity among his disciples. Let us now pray for this same gift for N. and N., for ourselves, for our families, and for all the world.

Response: Lord, grant that we may be one.

Reader(s): For the Church: that it may be a sign of unity and an instrument of peace in a divided and fragmented world. Let us pray.

For all who hold public office: that they may judge wisely and act fairly. Let us pray.

For N. and N.: that they may be totally committed to one another and to the task of building a good marriage. Let us pray.

That they may face the future with an unshakable faith in God and in each other. Let us pray.

For married couples: that they may be true and faithful to one another in spite of their weakness and the difficulties they encounter. Let us pray.

Let us now lay before God our own special needs, worries, and problems. [*Pause*] Let us pray.

President: Heavenly Father, our source of life, you know our weakness. May we reach out with joy to grasp your hand so that we can walk more readily in your ways. We ask this through Christ our Lord .

(Communion) Reflection

No. 9 or No. 10.

WEDDING ANNIVERSARIES

Introduction

We are led to believe that in this day and age to undertake a life-long commitment is, for the majority of people, completely out of the question. Indeed, the impression given is that most people are reluctant even to think about it.

But this impression is false. The fact is, in spite of everything, a great number of married couples still manage to do the unthinkable. They not only undertake the commitment to be faithful to one another for life but actually carry it out. But these seldom if ever get headlines in the media. The headlines are given over almost exclusively to the unfaithful ones.

Hence, one would expect that the Church would make a fuss over wedding anniversaries. Alas, such is far from being the case, which is a pity. The Church should be seen, not merely to demand lasting fidelity from couples, but to stand by them in carrying it out, encouraging them when they are struggling, and of course rejoicing and celebrating with them when they are successful.

The silver and golden anniversaries are looked upon as the really big milestones of the marriage journey, and normally are the only ones celebrated. But what is so magic about the numbers twenty-five and fifty? Why not, for instance, celebrate fifteen years, or twenty years of faithful love?

Most times it is left to the couple themselves, or to their family, whether or not to mark the occasion. While a celebration cannot be imposed, nevertheless, it could be suggested and encouraged. A parish community could, for instance, invite a number of couples who have been together for a good number of years, and ask them to renew their marriage promises at a public ceremony — a Sunday Mass perhaps? What a wonderful boost this would be for the couples and families involved. What a wonderful example it would be for couples not long married. What a powerful lesson for young people contemplating marriage.

In what follows four anniversary liturgies are given. In each case the number of years is left open. However, any of the liturgies in this book could, with a little tailoring, be adapted for such an occasion. Also included is a formula for the renewal of the marriage vows.

The anniversary celebration, done with some solemnity, could provide couples with a marvellous opportunity to repeat to one another again, after a quarter of a century, or whatever number of years, their vows of lasting love and fidelity.

RENEWAL OF MARRIAGE VOWS

This takes place after the homily. All stand.

President (addressing the husband and wife):
Dear friends, N. and N., on the day of your wedding you declared your love for one another in the presence of the Church's minister and the community. Christ has abundantly blessed your love, and will continue to do so. He consecrated you in baptism, and enriched and strengthened you in the sacrament of matrimony, so that you could carry out the duties of marriage in mutual and lasting fidelity.

The Church congratulates you and rejoices with you on reaching the .... milestone of your marriage journey. And so on this happy day I invite you to renew your marriage vows.

Husband:
N., my wife,
I want to renew the commitment I made to you on our wedding day.
I promise to be true to you in good times and in bad,
in sickness and in health.
I will love you and honour you
all the days of my life.

Wife:
N., my husband,
I want to renew the commitment I made to you on our wedding day.
I promise to be true to you in good times and in bad,
in sickness and in health.
I will love you and honour you
all the days of my life.

President:
N. and N., you have renewed your wedding vows in the presence of the Lord and this community. May the Lord in his goodness deepen your commitment to one another, and fill you both with his blessings.

Husband and wife may now give one another a sign of love.

The Prayer of the Faithful follows.

15. REMAINING FAITHFUL

Introduction

In the name of the Father and of the Son and of the Holy Spirit.

The grace of our Lord Jesus Christ, the love of God, and the fellowship of the Holy Spirit be with you all.

.... years ago to-day N. and N. made a solemn promise to one another. They promised to be faithful to one another in love for the rest of their lives. God blessed and sealed their promise, and by his grace has kept them faithful to it.

We are happy for them, and want to join with them in thanking God for all the graces and blessings he has given them during their married life.

Penitential Rite

We have all made promises of one kind and another. Let us pause to reflect on how easy it is to make a promise but how hard it is to keep it. [*Pause*]

Rare are the people who fully live up to their promises. Let us ask God, who alone is totally faithful, for forgiveness for our infidelities.

I confess to almighty God.

Prayers of the Mass: cf. Roman Missal.

Readings on page 112.

Homily

Peter had an orchard which produced excellent apples. One spring, in a burst of generosity, he promised to give some apples to his good friend, Paul. So when autumn came around he filled a sack with apples, and on a bright morning put the sack on his back, and set out for the house of his friend.

But he had not gone far when he discovered that the sack was mighty heavy. Reluctantly he removed a quantity of the apples. This done, he resumed his journey. However, the sack was still heavy and was hurting his shoulder. So once again he lightened it. Then he made up his mind that there would be no more concessions to his weakness.

But he bargained without considering certain facts. He had forgotten that the house of his friend was a whole day's journey away. He had also forgotten to bring food with him. Now a gnawing hunger began to torment him. On top of all these difficulties the day was unbearably hot.

Several times he thought seriously about turning back. The thing that kept him going was the promise he had made to his friend. In all his difficulties the only thing he could turn to for a little relief were the apples. Some of these he ate. Others he exchanged for food or cigarettes with strangers he met along the way.

To make a long story short, when he finally reached his friend's house, he looked into the sack and was horrified to discover that there was only a handful of apples left. He was at a loss as to know how to explain this to his friend.

We have all made promises. While it is easy to make a promise, it is not always easy to carry it out. Like the man with the bag of apples, we learn a number of lessons in attempting to deliver on our promises.

On the day we make a promise we have perhaps little or no idea what that promise entails. But as we go through life, the full implications of it are gradually revealed to us. We learn, too, that we are self-divided. Each of us is a mixture of strength and weakness, courage and cowardice, generosity and selfishness. And we discover the meaning of friendship. Friendship is not just a nice feeling among people who get along well together, but something which calls for a readiness to make sacrifices and undergo pain. I believe that anyone who has made a significant promise could vouch for the truth of these things.

... years ago N. and N. made a very significant promise to one another. They promised to share with one another, not a miserable bag of apples, but the whole of their lives. They vowed to make a gift of their whole selves to one another. I am sure that on looking back over the years that have passed since the day they made their solemn promises, they would agree with the main thrust of the story of the bag of apples.

During those years they have discovered what it was they promised each other on their wedding day. They have also learned a lot about themselves. And they have undoubtedly learned that true love, though the most beautiful and necessary thing in the world, is a costly thing. Yet, in spite of everything, they are still on the road, and still paying up to one another.

Every promise has to be remade, not once, but many times. This celebration gives them an opportunity, not only to thank God for his fidelity to them, but also to thank one another, and to remake those solemn promises they made ... years ago.

"There is no growth except in the fulfilment of one's obligations." (Antoine de Saint Exupery).

"Hell is the suffering of those who can no longer love." (Dostoyevsky).

Prayer of the Faithful

President: God, our Father, is our source of life and strength. In spite of our infidelities, he remains faithful to us. Let us now pray earnestly to him so that we may be able to persevere on the hard but joyful path of faithfulness.

Response: Lord, hear our prayer.

Reader(s): For all the followers of Christ: that they may be steadfast in faith, joyful in hope, and untiring in love. Let us pray to the Lord.

For all who hold public office: that they may be faithful to their commitments and responsibilities. Let us pray to the Lord.

For N. and N.: that God may keep them faithful in their love for one another. Let us pray to the Lord.

For all here present: that God may bless us with a generous and faithful love so that we may be true to our promises. Let us pray to the Lord.

For the victims of broken promises: that their wounds may be healed. Let us pray to the Lord.

For the faithful departed, especially those near and dear to us: that they may enjoy the fullness of eternal life. Let us pray to the Lord.

President: Heavenly Father, grant that what we have said with our lips, we may believe with our hearts, and practise with our lives. We make this prayer through Christ our Lord.

Communion Reflection

No. 15 or No. 16.

16. THE LAMP STILL BURNS

Introduction

In the name of the Father and of the Son and of the Holy Spirit.
The grace and peace of God our Father and the Lord Jesus Christ be with you.

This is a happy occasion. This is a bright day, not only for N. and N., but for all of us who love them. What makes this day a bright one is the fact that the lamp of their love, which was lit .... years ago, is still burning. This is a cause for joy and thanksgiving.

Penitential Rite

The lamp of human love is a frail one. We cannot always depend on it. But there is one lamp the never goes out. This is the lamp of God's love for us. Let us pause to reflect for a moment on this wonderful truth. [*Pause*]

Let us ask the Lord's forgiveness for the fact that we sometimes allow the lamp of love to grow dim or perhaps to go out altogether.

I confess to almighty God.

Prayers of the Mass: cf. Roman Missal.

Readings on page 114.

Homily

.... years ago a lamp began to shine in the lives of N. and N.— the lamp of their mutual love. On the day of their wedding this lamp was raised on high and placed on a lampstand. Thus it shed its light, not only into their lives, but also into the lives of their relatives and friends.

Thanks to modern technology, it is now possible to have a lamp that never goes out. The human lamp, however, has not changed much over the centuries. It remains a frail, imperfect, and unreliable thing.

Nevertheless, practically all marriages begin very brightly. But this is part of the problem. They begin not just with high expectations, but with impossible expectations. We expect our partner to give us continuous friendship. And what happens? Problems arise. Routine and boredom set in. Disillusionment rears its ugly head. The net result is that the light begins to grow dim.

I am sure that over the years N. and N. have had their share of joys and sorrows, satisfactions and disappointments. Nevertheless, in spite of everything, the lamp of their love is still burning.

They have much that they can look back on with gratitude and satisfaction. Nothing can match the treasury of common memories, of trials endured together, of difficulties faced and overcome together, of quarrels and reconciliations. The greater the difficulties and disappointments that are successfully met, the greater the joy and peace which fidelity brings.

But in the final analysis, only God is fully faithful. In his love for us, he has bound himself to us in a covenant of friendship. He is faithful to this covenant forever.

As for us, we are plagued by weakness and dogged by infidelity. But God understands our weakness. He pardons our infidelities. He heals our love when we fall. He saves its precious light from extinction when the cold winds of selfishness, disillusionment, and cynicism assail it.

N. and N. are no doubt very different people from the people they were on their wedding day. We pray that God will not only keep them faithful to one another, but help them to remain truly in love with each other. To stay in love means to love each other, not as they were, but as they are.

"All that we love deeply becomes a part of us." (Helen Keller).

"In the evening of life we shall be examined on love." (St John of the Cross).

Prayer of the Faithful

President: Let us pray that the lamp of love which N. and N. lit in our midst .... years ago, will continue to illumine their lives and the lives of all of us.

Response: Lord, hear our prayer.

Reader(s): For all Christians: that through their good deeds they may cause the light of Christ's love to shine brightly in a world darkened by indifference and despair. Let us pray to the Lord.

For all those who hold public office: that through their

wisdom and integrity they may bring light to a world darkened by war and want. Let us pray to the Lord.

For N. and N.: that they may continue to walk in the bright light of a true and faithful love for one another. Let us pray to the Lord.

For all of us, married or single: that we may walk in the light of goodness and faithfulness. Let us pray to the Lord.

For those who have to walk in the darkness of broken promises: that they may not lose heart. Let us pray to the Lord.

For the faithful departed, especially our own relatives and friends: that God may call them into his kingdom of light and peace. Let us pray to the Lord.

President: Heavenly Father, may the radiance of your unfailing love light up our hearts, and bring us safely through the shadows of this world until we reach our homeland of everlasting light. We ask this through Christ our Lord.

Communion Reflection

No. 16 or No. 17.

17. STILL ON THE CHOSEN ROAD

Introduction

In the name of the Father and of the Son and of the Holy Spirit.

The grace of our Lord Jesus Christ, the love of God, and the fellowship of the Holy Spirit be with you all.

.... years ago N. and N. linked their lives together. They vowed that from that day on they would travel the road of life together as husband and wife. Thanks be to God, they are still together. We are happy for them. The whole Church is happy for them.

Penitential Rite

Whether married or single, we all are on the mysterious journey of life, a journey that can never be re-traced. Let us pause for a moment to reflect on how we feel about it. [*Pause*]

Perhaps we are disappointed, or confused, or hurt, or guilty. Let us turn to God who loves each of us as a dear son or daughter, and ask him for pardon, healing, and strength.

Lord, you were sent to heal the broken-hearted. Lord, have mercy.

You came to call sinners to repentance. Christ, have mercy.

You plead for us now at the right hand of the Father. Lord, have mercy.

Prayers of the Mass: cf. the Roman Missal.

Readings on page 116.

Homily

Marriage could be compared to a journey. When a man and woman get married they commit themselves to a common journey. This journey almost invariably begins with great expectations and in a blaze of joy. But what happens? Difficulties arise. Problems occur. Boredom sets in. The result is that we are disappointed, maybe even disillusioned.

However, there is no need to panic. All this is natural, and happens in every walk of life, even in the most sacred professions and vocations. A young doctor on beginning his practice treats his patients as if they were his own children. But pretty soon this changes due to the pressures of the daily grind. A priest celebrates his first Mass with at least one foot in heaven. But before a year has passed he is well and truly back down to earth.

I am sure that N. and N. can identify with this. No doubt, in the years they have been together, they have had their joys and sorrows, satisfactions and disappointments, trials and difficulties. Their journey has been more difficult than they had envisaged. However, a difficult journey is not necessarily a misfortune. In fact it can turn out to be a blessing. The very difficulties we have encountered and overcome, the sacrifices we have made for one another, far from loosening the bond with which we linked our lives on our wedding day, can have the effect of strengthening and cementing it.

N. and N. have reached the ... milestone of their common journey. We are happy for them. The Church is happy for them and congratulates them. This happy occasion provides them with an opportunity to renew their vows to one another. Every choice in life has to be re-made, not once, but many times, if we are to remain true to it. Each day a new part of the chosen path opens up before us. This is good because it makes for change. But it also provides a challenge. We have to say "yes" to the new as we have said "yes" to the old.

It is only as we go along that the full implications of our original choice are gradually brought home to us. Hence, we have to go on repeating and renewing that original "yes" we said to one another all those years ago.

It is also an opportunity for them to let go of any unnecessary baggage they may have picked up along the way — regrets for what might have been, bitterness over hurts suffered, guilt over mistakes made, and so on. Gratitude for what they have been able to achieve, forgiveness for what has gone wrong — these will help them to go forward with renewed spirit.

Fidelity brings its own rewards in terms of inner peace and happiness. We pray that their relationship will go on deepening and ripening, and that God will help them to persevere in their chosen path — the path of faithful love.

"The happiness that comes from easy victories, from total fulfilment of desire, from success, from feeling completely gorged — that is suffering." (Solzhenitsyn).

"Today's greatest deception is an unattainable happiness." (Michel Quoist).

Prayer of the Faithful

President: It is from God that we come when we enter this world, and it is to him that we go when we leave it. Let us turn to him to seek his guidance and grace so that we may walk more readily in his ways.

Response: Lord, hear us in your love.

Reader(s): For all Christians: that they may follow Christ with generosity and steadfastness. We pray in faith.

For all government leaders: that they may work to build a world free from war and hunger so that all people may be able to live in freedom and dignity. We pray in faith.

For N. and N.: that the journey they began ... years ago in faith, may continue in hope and love. We pray in faith.

For those who are lost on the highway of life: that they may find their way. We pray in faith.

For all here present: that each of us may derive an increase of hope from taking part in this celebration. We pray in faith.

For all our departed relatives and friends, and for all who have died in the peace of Christ: that they may enjoy the fullness of eternal life. We pray in faith.

President: Heavenly Father, grant us in all our tasks your help, in all our doubts your guidance, in all our weaknesses your strength, in all our sorrows your consolation, and in all our dangers your protection. We ask this through Christ our Lord.

Communion Reflection

No. 17 or No. 14.

18. THE BOND STILL HOLDS

Introduction

In the name of the Father and of the Son and of the Holy Spirit.
The grace and peace of God our Father and the Lord Jesus Christ be
with you.

.... years ago at this time N. and N. tied the knot, as we say. They bound
their lives and destinies together by a bond which God blessed, sealed and
wanted to remain. And by the grace of God, and their cooperation with
that grace, the bond still holds.

We are celebrating this Mass to thank God for the graces he has given
them during the past .... years, and also for the example of faithfulness he
has given us through them.

Penitential Rite

In one way ar another all our lives are bound together, so much so that
we have a profound influence on one another for good or ill. Let us reflect
on this for a moment. [*Pause*]

We are not always as helpful or as loyal to one another as we could be.
Let us therefore ask the Lord's forgiveness.

I confess to almighty God.

Prayers of the Mass: cf. the Roman Missal.

Readings on page 118.

Homily

.... years ago N. and N. bound their lives together in the sacrament of
marriage. The bond of marriage is not meant to be a mere legal tie. Nor
is it meant to be a fetter or chain, making prisoners out of one or both
partners. It is meant to be a bond of love. Now the essential act which
creates a bond of love between two or more people is sacrifice.

Only that man understands what a farm is who has sacrificed part of
himself to that farm. This sacrifice creates a bond between him and his

farm. Only that woman understands what a home is who has worked to make it beautiful. It is precisely because of the sacrifices she has made for her house that the love of it fills her heart. In the same way, only that couple who have sacrificed themselves for one another understand what marriage is. For them the marriage bond is truly a bond of love.

Solzhenitsyn, the Russian writer, experienced war and imprisonment for his country. But he tells how this experience, far from impoverishing him, greatly enriched him. "I must admit," he says, "that before my experience of war and prison I didn't have much faith in friends, particularly in the business of laying down one's life for them. But the war changed all this. During the war we drank to friendship and love. In roadside ditches, in flooded trenches, in the ruins of gutted houses we learned the value of a tin of soup, an hour of quiet, the meaning of true friendship, the meaning of life itself."

But he goes on to say that on returning to civilian life the same soldiers were stunned by what they found. They had been purified by the nearness of death, but when they got home they were appalled by the callous, often totally unscrupulous way in which people treated one another.

The point being made is this: it is not an easy life but a difficult life which creates a deep bond between people. The very difficulties encountered, and the sacrifices made for one another, are what fashion and strengthen the bond between them. These are precisely the things out of which friendship and loyalty are born.

During the past .... years no doubt N. and N. have had their ups and downs, joys and sorrows, successes and failures, satisfactions and disappointments. They have travelled a long way and been through a lot together. Yet, by the grace of God and their cooperation with that grace, the bond has held. We pray that the things they have suffered together and the sacrifices they have made for one another, will strengthen this bond.

This ceremony gives them an opportunity to commit themselves once more to one another. God blessed them on their wedding day. He blesses them again today. May they go forward in confidence, knowing that his grace will keep them faithful in the future as it did in the past.

"Trustworthiness is the most constant virtue which is not acquired or lost with the years." (Primo Levi).

"There is no comradeship except through union in the same high effort." (Antoine de Saint Exupery).

Prayer of the Faithful

President: Left to ourselves, we cannot do the will of God. So let us turn with confidence to God, and ask him in his gentle mercy to guide our wayward hearts.

Response: Lord, graciously hear us.

Reader(s): For the Church: that God may bind its members together so that they might form a true community, producing the fruits of unity and peace. Lord, hear us.

For world leaders: that God may bless them with wisdom and integrity so that they may bind the human family together in ties of friendship and cooperation. Lord, hear us.

For N. and N.: that God, who blessed and sealed their union on their wedding day, may bless them today and strengthen the bond by which their lives and destinies are joined together. Lord, hear us.

For marriages that have broken down: that God may heal the wounds which result from every breakdown. Lord, hear us.

For all gathered here: that we may be true and loyal friends to one another. Lord, hear us.

That all those whom we loved in this life, but whom death has taken from us, may come to a place of refreshment, light, and peace. Lord hear us.

President: Heavenly Father, fill our hearts with your love. Give us the grace to rise above our human weaknesses, and keep us faithful to you and to one another. We ask this through Christ our Lord.

Communion Reflection

No. 15 or No. 14

Readings

1. WHERE LOVE IS, GOD IS

FIRST READING   Sir 6:6-12, 14-15

There is a false friend and a true friend. A false friend is worthless, a true friend
is a treasure.

A Reading from the Book of Sirach
Let those that are at peace with you be many,
but let your advisers be one in a thousand.
When you gain a friend, gain him through testing,
and do not trust him hasily.
For there is a friend who is such at his own convenience,
but will not stand by you in your day of trouble.
And there is a friend who changes into an enemy,
and will disclose a quarrel to your disgrace.
And there is a friend who is a table companion
but will not stand by you in your day of trouble.
In your prosperity he will make himself your equal,
and be bold with your servants;
but if you are brought low he will turn against you,
and will hide himself from your presence.
A faithful friend is a sturdy shelter:
he that has found one has found a treasure.
There is nothing so precious as a faithful friend,
and no scales can measure his excellence.
    This is the word of the Lord.

Responsorial Psalm   Ps 102(103):8,10-14,17-18

Response: The Lord is compassion and love.

    The Lord is compassion and love
    slow to anger and rich in mercy.
    He does not treat us according to our sins
    nor repay us according to our faults. **R.**

For as the heavens are high above the earth
so strong is his love for those who fear him.
As far as the east is from the west
so far does he remove our sins. **R.**

As a father has compassion on his children,
the Lord has pity on those who fear him;
for he knows of what we are made,
he remembers that we are dust. **R.**

The love of the Lord is everlasting
upon those who fear him;
his justice reaches out to children's children
when they keep his covenant in truth. **R.**

SECOND READING   1 Jn 4:7-12

Those who love, know God because God is love.

A reading from the first letter of Saint John
Let us love one another; for love is of God, and he who loves is born of
God and knows God. He who does not love does not know God; for God
is love.

In this the love of God was made manifest among us, that God sent his
only Son into the world, so that we might live through him. In this is love,
not that we loved God but that he loved us and sent his Son to be the
expiation for our sins.

If God so loved us, we also ought to love one another. No man has ever
seen God; if we love one another, God abides in us and his love is
perfected in us.

This is the word of the Lord.

Gospel Acclamation   Jn 15:12

Alleluia, alleluia! (*Lent:* Praise to you, Lord Jesus Christ).
This is my commandment:
Love one another as I have loved you,
says the Lord.
Alleluia! (*Lent:* Praise to you, Lord Jesus Christ).

GOSPEL   Mk 10:6-9

Christ teaches that the marriage bond comes from God and is indissoluble.

A reading from the holy Gospel according to Mark
Jesus said:
"From the beginning of creation, 'God made them male and female.
For this reason a man shall leave his father and mother and be joined to
his wife, and the two shall become one.' So they are no longer two but one.
What therefore God has joined together, let not man put asunder."
This is the Gospel of the Lord.

2. LOVE IS ... *I*

FIRST READING   Gen 2:18-24

In and through marriage, God intends man and woman to be companions and
helpers to one another, so that in a sense they are no longer two but one.

A reading from the Book of Genesis
Then the Lord God said:
"It is not good that the man should be alone; I will make him a helper
fit for him." So out of the ground the Lord God formed every beast of the
field and every bird of the air, and brought them to the man to see what
he would call them; and whatever the man called every living creature,
that was its name.

The man gave names to all cattle, and to the birds of the air, and to
every beast of the field; but for the man there was not found a helper fit
for him. So the Lord God caused a deep sleep to fall upon the man, and
while he slept took one of his ribs and closed up its place with flesh; and
the rib which the Lord God had taken from the man he made into a woman
and brought her to the man. Then the man said, "This at last is bone of my
bones and flesh of my flesh; she shall be called Woman, because she was
taken out of Man."

Therefore a man leaves his father and his mother and cleaves to his
wife, and they become one flesh.
This is the word of the Lord.

Responsorial Psalm   Ps 137(138):1-3,6-7.

Response: Your love, O Lord, is eternal.

I thank you, Lord, with all my heart,
you have heard the words of my mouth.
Before the angels I will bless you.
I will adore before your holy temple. **R.**

I thank you for your faithfulness and love
which excel all we ever knew of you.
On the day I called, you answered;
you increased the strength of my soul. **R.**

The Lord is high yet he looks on the lowly
and the haughty he knows from afar.
Though I walk in the midst of affliction
you give me life and frustrate my foes. **R.**

You stretch out your hand and save me,
your hand will do all things for me.
Your love, O Lord, is eternal,
discard not the work of your hands. **R.**

SECOND READING   1 Cor 13:1-7

No one ever so stressed the importance of love, or described it better, than St Paul.

A reading from the first letter of St. Paul to the Corinthians
If I speak in the tongues of men and of angels, but have not love, I am a noisy gong or a clanging cymbal.

And if I have prophetic powers, and understand all mysteries and all knowledge, and if I have all faith, so as to remove mountains, but have not love, I am nothing.

If I give away all I have, and if I deliver my body to be burned, but have not love, I gain nothing.

Love is patient and kind;
love is not jealous or boastful;
it is not arrogant or rude.
Love does not insist on its own way;
it is not irritable or resentful;
it does not rejoice at wrong, but rejoices in the right.

Love bears all things,
believes all things,
hopes all things.
Love never ends.
This is the word of the Lord.

Gospel Acclamation   Jn 15:9

Alleluia, alleluia! (*Lent:* Praise to you, Lord Jesus Christ).
As the Father has loved me,
so I have loved you;
abide in my love, says the Lord.
Alleluia! (*Lent:* Praise to you, Lord Jesus Christ).

GOSPEL   Jn 13:34-35

Christ urges his disciples to love one another as he has loved them.

A reading from the holy Gospel according to John
Jesus said to his disciples:
"A new commandment I give to you, that you love one another; even
as I have loved you, that you also love one another.
"By this all men will know that you are my disciples, if you have love
for one another."
This is the Gospel of the Lord.

3. LOVE IS ... *II*

FIRST READING   Gen 1:26-28,31

God made man and woman for one another. The bond of marriage means that in
a sense they are no longer two but one.

A Reading from the Book of Genesis
Then God said:
"Let us make man in our image, after our likeness; and let them have
dominion over the fish of the sea, and over the birds of the air, and over

the cattle, and over all the earth and over every creeping thing that creeps upon the earth."

So God created man in his own image, in the image of God he created him; male and female he created them. And God blessed them, and God said to them, "Be fruitful and multiply, and fill the earth and subdue it; and have dominion over the fish of the sea and over the birds of the air and over every living thing that moves upon the earth."

And God saw everything that he had made, and behold it was very good.

This is the word of the Lord.

Responsorial Psalm   Ps 102(103):8,10-14,17-18.

Response: The Lord is compassion and love.

The Lord is compassion and love,
slow to anger and rich in mercy.
He does not treat us according to our sins
nor repay us according to our faults. **R.**

For as the heavens are high above the earth
so strong is his love for those who fear him.
As far as the east is from the west
so far does he remove our sins. **R.**

As a father has compassion on his children,
the Lord has pity on those who fear him;
for he knows of what we are made,
he remembers that we are dust. **R.**

The love of the Lord is everlasting
upon those who fear him;
his justice reaches out to children's children
when they keep his covenant in truth. **R.**

SECOND READING   1 Cor 13:1-7

No one ever so stressed the importance of love, or described it better, than St Paul.

A reading from the first letter of St Paul to the Corinthians.
If I speak in the tongues of men and of angels, but have not love, I am a noisy gong or a clanging cymbal.

And if I have prophetic powers, and understand all mysteries and all knowledge, and if I have all faith, so as to remove mountains, but have not love, I am nothing.

If I give away all I have, and if I deliver my body to be burned, but have not love, I gain nothing.

Love is patient and kind;
love is not jealous or boastful;
it is not arrogant or rude.
Love does not insist on its own way;
it is not irritable or resentful;
it does not rejoice at wrong, but rejoices in the right.
Love bears all things,
believes all things,
hopes all things.
Love never ends.
This is the word of the Lord.

Gospel Acclamation   Jn 15:13.

Alleluia, alleluia! (*Lent:* Praise to you, Lord Jesus Christ).
Greater love has no man than this,
that a man lay down his life for his friends,
says the Lord.
Alleluia! (*Lent:* Praise to you, Lord Jesus Christ).

GOSPEL   Jn 15:9-12

Christ urges his disciples to love one another as he has loved them.

A reading from the holy Gospel according to John.
Jesus said to his disciples:

"As the Father has loved me, so have I loved you; abide in my love. If you keep my commandments, you will abide in my love, just as I have kept my Father's commandments and abide in his love. These things I have spoken to you, that my joy may be in you, and that your joy may be full.

"This is my commandment, that you love one another as I have loved you."

This is the Gospel of the Lord.

4. THE LAMP OF LOVE

A poem which sings the praises of lover.

A reading from the Song of Songs

First Version: (One reader).

My beloved speaks and says to me:
"Arise, my love, my fair one, and come away;
for lo, the winter is past,
the rain is over and gone.
The flowers appear on the earth,
the time of singing has come,
and the voice of the turtle-dove is heard in our land.
The fig tree puts forth its figs,
and the vines are in blossom;
they give forth fragrance.
Arise, my love, my fair one, and come away.
Let me see your face,
let me hear your voice,
for your voice is sweet,
and your face is comely."
My beloved is mine and I am his. He said to me:
"Set me as a seal upon your heart,
as a seal upon your arm;
for love is strong as death.
Many waters cannot quench love,
neither can floods drown it.
If a man offered for love all the wealth of his house,
it would be utterly scorned."
My beloved is mine and I am his.
     This is the word of the Lord.

Second Version: (Bride and bridegroom in dialogue.)

> *Bride:*   Your love is better than wine,
>   your name is oil poured out.
>   Draw me after you, let us make haste.

Bridegroom: Arise, my love, my fair one, and come away;
for lo, the winter is past,
the rain is over and gone.
The flowers appear on the earth,
the time of singing has come
and the voice of the turtle-dove is heard in our land.
The fig tree puts forth its figs,
and the vines are in blossom;
they give forth fragrance.
Arise, my love, my fair one, and come away.
Let me see your face,
Let me hear your voice,
for your voice is sweet,
and your face is comely.

Bride: My beloved, you are mine and I am yours.

Bridgegroom: Set me as a seal upon your heart,
as a seal upon your arm;
for love is strong as death.
Many waters cannot quench love,
neither can floods drown it.
If a man offered for love all the wealth of his house,
it would be utterly scorned.

Bride: My beloved, you are mine and I am yours.

Both: This is the word of the Lord.

Responsorial Psalm   Ps 26(27):1,4,10,13,14.

Response: The Lord is my light and my help.

The Lord is my light and my help;
whom, shall I fear?
The Lord is the stronghold of my life;
before whom shall I shrink? **R**

There is one thing I ask of the Lord,
for this I long,
to live in the house of the Lord
all the days of my life. **R.**

Do not abandon or forsake me,
O God my help.

Though father and mother forsake me,
the Lord will receive me. **R.**

I am sure I shall see the Lord's goodness
in the land of the living.
Hope in him, hold firm and take heart.
Hope in the Lord. **R.**

SECOND READING   1 Jn 2:7-11

To love is to walk in the light; not to love is to walk in darkness.

A reading from the first letter of St John
Beloved, I am writing you no new commandment, but an old commandment which you had from the beginning; the old commandment is the
word which you have heard.

Yet I am writing you a new commandment, which is true in him and
in you, because the darkness is passing away and the true light is already
shining.

He who say s he is in the light and hates his brother is in the darkness
still. He who loves his brother abides in the light, and in it there is no cause
for stumbling. But he who hates his brother is in the darkness and walks
in the darkness, and does not know where he is going, because the
darkness has blinded his eyes.

This is the word of the Lord.

Gospel Acclamation   1 Jn 3:18

Alleluia, alleluia! (Lent: Praise to you, Lord Jesus Christ).
Let us not love in word or speech
but in deed and in truth.
Alleluia! (Lent: Praise to you, Lord Jesus Christ).

GOSPEL   Mt 5:13-16

Christ urges his followers to let the light of their good deeds shine for all to see,
while giving the glory to God.

A reading from the holy Gospel according to Matthew
Jesus said to his disciples:

"You are the salt of the earth; but if salt has lost its taste, how shall its
saltiness be restored? It is no longer good for anything except to be thrown

out and trodden under foot by men.

"You are the light of the world. A city set on a hill cannot be hid. Nor do men light a lamp and put it under a bushel, but on a stand, and it gives light to all in the house. Let your light shine before men, that they may see your good works and give glory to your Father who is in heaven."

This is the Gospel of the Lord.

5. WHEN THE WINE RUNS OUT

FIRST READING   Gen 1:26-28,31

God made man and woman for one another. The bond of marriage means that in a sense they are no longer two but one.

A reading from the book of Genesis

Then God said:

"Let us make man in our image, after our likeness; and let them have dominion over the fish of the sea, and over the birds of the air, and over the cattle, and over all the earth, and over every creeping thing that creeps upon the earth."

So God created man in his own image, in the image of God he created him; male and female he created them. And God blessed them, and God said to them, "Be fruitful and multiply, and fill the earth and subdue it; and have dominion over the fish of the sea and the birds of the air and over every living thing that moves upon the earth."

And God saw everything that he had made, and behold it was very good.

This is the word of the Lord.

Responsorial Psalm   Ps 32(33):12-15,18-22

Response: May your love be upon us, O Lord,
                  as we place all our hope in you.

They are happy, whose God is the Lord,
the people he has chosen as his own.
From the heavens the Lord looks forth,
he sees all the children of men. **R.**

From the place where he dwells he gazes
on all the dwellers on the earth,
he who shapes the hearts of them all
and considers all their deeds. **R.**

The Lord looks on those who revere him,
on those who hope in his love,
to rescue their souls from death,
to keep them alive in famine. **R.**

Our soul is waiting for the Lord.
The Lord is our help and our shield.
In him do our hearts find joy.
We trust in his holy name. **R.**

SECOND READING   1 Cor 13:1-7

No one ever so stressed the importance of love, or described it better, than St Paul.

A reading from the first letter of St Paul to the Corinthians
If I speak in the tongues of men and of angels, but have not love, I am a
noisy gong or a clanging cymbal.

And if I have prophetic powers, and understand all mysteries and all
knowledge, and if I have all faith, so as to remove mountains, but have
not love, I am nothing.

If I give away all I have, and if I deliver my body to be burned, but have
not love, I gain nothing.

Love is patient and kind;
love is not jealous or boastful;
it is not arrogant or rude.
Love does not insist on its own way;
it is not irritable or resentful;
it does not rejoice at wrong, but rejoices in the right.
Love bears all things,
believes all things,
hopes all things.
Love never ends.
This is the word of the Lord.

Gospel Acclamation   Jn 13:35

Alleluia, alleluia! (*Lent:* Praise to you, Lord Jesus Christ).
By this all men will know that you are my disciples,
if you have love for one another,
says the Lord.
Alleluia! (*Lent:* Praise to you, Lord Jesus Christ).

GOSPEL   Jn 2:1-11

This tells the story of the first sign given by Jesus, when at a wedding he changed
water into wine.

A reading from the holy Gospel according to John
There was a marriage at Cana in Galilee, and the mother of Jesus was
there; Jesus also was invited to the marriage, with his disciples. When the
wine failed, the mother of Jesus said to him, "They have no wine." And
Jesus said to her, "O woman, what have you to do with me? My hour has
not yet come." His mother said to the servants, "Do whatever he tells
you."

Now six stone jars were standing there, for the Jewish rites of
purification, each holding twenty or thirty gallons. Jesus said to them,
"Fill the jars with water." And they filled them up to the brim. He said to
them, "Now draw some out, and take it to the steward of the feast." So they
took it.

When the steward of the feast tasted the water now become wine, and
did not know where it came from (though the servants who had drawn the
water knew), the steward of the feast called the bridegroom and said to
him, "Every man serves the good wine first; and when men have drunk
freely, then the poor wine; but you have kept the good wine until now."

This, the first of his signs, Jesus did at Cana in Galilee, and manifested
his glory; and his disciples believed in him.

This is the Gospel of the Lord.

6. GIVING ONE'S SOLEMN WORD

FIRST READING   Sir 6:6-12,14-16

There is a false friend and a true friend. A false friend is worthless; a true friend is a treasure.

A reading from the book of Sirach
Let those that are at peace with you be many,
but let your advisers be one in a thousand.
When you gain a friend, gain him through testing,
and do not trust him hastily.
For there is a friend who is such at his own convenience,
but will not stand by you in your day of trouble.
And there is a friend who changes into an enemy,
and will disclose a quarrel to your disgrace.
And there is a friend who is a table companion,
but will not stand by you in your day of trouble.
In your prosperity he will make himself your equal,
and be bold with your servants;
but if you are brought low he will turn against you,
and will hide himself from your presence.
A faithful friend is a sturdy shelter;
he that has found one has found a treasure.
There is nothing so precious as a faithful friend,
and no scales can measure his excellence.
    This is the word of the Lord.

Responsorial Psalm   Ps 102(103):8,10-14,17-18

Response: The Lord is compassion and love.

   The Lord is compassion and love,
   slow to anger and rich in mercy.
   He does not treat us according to our sins
   nor repay us according to our faults. **R.**

   For as the heavens are high above the earth
   so strong is his love for those who fear him.
   As far as the east is from the west
   so far does he remove our sins. **R.**

As a father has compassion on his children,
the Lord has pity on those who fear him;
for he knows of what we are made,
he remembers that we are dust. **R.**

The love of the Lord is everlasting
upon those who fear him;
his justice reaches out to children's children
when they keep his covenant in truth. **R.**

SECOND READING   1 Jn 3:18-24

Christ's great commandment is the commandment to love one another. However, it is not good enough to love in word; we must also love in deed and in truth

A reading from the first Letter of Saint John
Little children, let us not love one another in word or speech but in deed and in truth.

By this we shall know that we are of the truth, and reassure our hearts before him whenever our hearts condemn us; for God is greater than our hearts, and he knows everything.

Beloved, if our hearts do not condemn us, we have confidence before God; and we receive from him whatever we ask, because we keep his commandments and do what pleases him.

And this is his commandment, that we should believe in the name of his Son Jesus Christ and love one another, just as he has commanded us. All who keep his commandments abide in him, and he in them. And by this we know that he abides in us, by the Spirit which he has given us.

This is the word of the Lord.

Gospel Acclamation   1 Jn 4:7-8

Alleluia, alleluia! (*Lent:* Praise to you, Lord Jesus Christ).
He who loves is born of God
and knows God,
for God is love.
Alleluia! (*Lent:* Praise to you, Lord Jesus Christ).

GOSPEL   Mt 19:3-6

Christ teaches that the bond of marriage comes from God and is indissoluble.

A reading from the holy Gospel according to Matthew
Some Pharisees came up to Jesus and tested him by asking, "Is it lawful to divorce one's wife for any cause?"

He answered, "Have you not read that he who made them from the beginning made them male and female, and said, "For this reason a man shall leave his father and mother and be joined to his wife, and the two shall become one."

"So they are no longer two but one.What therefore God has joined together, let no man put asunder."

This is the Gospel of the Lord.

7. WHEN TWO ROADS MEET

FIRST READING   Gen 1:26-28,31

God made man and woman for one another. The bond of marriage means that in a sense they are no longer two but one.

A reading from the book of Genesis
Then God said:

"Let us make man in our image, after our likeness; and let them have dominion over the fish of the sea, and over the birds of the air, and over the cattle, and over all the earth, and over every creeping thing that creeps upon the earth."

So God created man in his own image, in the image of God he created him; male and female he created them. And God blessed them, and God said to them, "Be fruitful and multiply, and fill the earth and subdue it; and have dominion over the fish of the sea and over the birds of the air and over every living thing that moves upon the earth."

And God saw everything that he had made, and behold it was very good.

This is the word of the Lord.

Responsorial Psalm   Ps 120(121):1-8

Response: My help shall come from the Lord
                who made heaven and earth

I lift up my eyes to the mountains:
from where shall come my help?
My help shall come from the Lord
who made heaven and earth. **R**.

May he never allow you to stumble.
Let him sleep not, your guard.
No, he sleeps not nor slumbers,
Israel's guard. **R**.

The Lord is your guard and your shade;
at your right side he stands.
By day the sun shall not smite you
nor the moon in the night. **R**.

The Lord will guard you from evil,
he will guard your soul.
The Lord will guard your going and coming
both now and for ever. **R**.

SECOND READING   1 Cor 13:1-7

No one ever so stressed the importance of love or described it better, than St Paul.

A reading from the first letter of St Paul to the Corinthians
If I speak in the tongues of men and of angels, but have not love, I am a
noisy gong or a clanging cymbal.
    And if I have prophetic powers, and understand all mysteries and all
knowledge, and if I have all faith, so as to remove mountains, but have
not love, I am nothing.
    If I give away all I have, and if I deliver my body to be burned, but have
not love, I gain nothing.
    Love is patient and kind;
    love is not jealous or boastful;
    it is not arrogant or rude.
    Love does not insist on its own way;
    it is not irritable or resentful;
    it does not rejoice at wrong, but rejoices in the right.

Love bears all things,
believes all things,
hopes all things.
Love never ends.
This is the word of the Lord.

Gospel Acclamation   Jn 15:9

Alleluia, alleluia! (*Lent:* Praise to you, Lord Jesus Christ).
As the Father has loved me,
so I have loved you;
abide in my love,
says the Lord.
Alleluia! (*Lent:* Praise to you, Lord Jesus Christ).

GOSPEL   Jn 13:34-35

Christ urges his disciples to love one another as he has loved them.

A reading from the holy Gospel according to John.
Jesus said to his disciples:
"A new commandment I give to you, that you love one another; even as I have loved you, that you also love one another.
"By this all men will know that you are my disciples, if you have love for one another."
This is the Gospel of the Lord.

8. BUILDING A RELATIONSHIP

FIRST READING   Sir 6:6-12,14-15

There is a true friend and a false friend. A false friend is worthless, a true friend is a treasure.

A reading from the book of Sirach
Let those that are at peace with you be many,
but let your advisers be one in a thousand.
When you gain a friend, gain him through testing,

and do not trust him hastily.
For there is a friend who is such at his own convenience,
but will not stand by you in your day of trouble.
And there is a friend who changes into an enemy,
and will disclose a quarrel to your disgrace.
And there is a friend who is a table companion,
but will not stand by you in your day of trouble.
In your prosperity he will make himself your equal,
and be bold with your servants;
but if you are brought low he will turn against you,
and will hide himself from your presence.
A faithful friend is a sturdy shelter:
he that has found one has found a treasure.
There is nothing so precious as a faithful friend,
and no scales can measure his excellence.
　　This is the word of the Lord.

Responsorial Psalm   Ps 99(100):1-5

Response: The Lord is faithful from age to age.

Cry out with joy to the Lord, all the earth.
Serve the Lord with gladness.
Come before him, singing for joy. **R.**

Know that he, the Lord, is God.
He made us, we belong to him,
we are his people, the sheep of his flock. **R.**

Go within his gates, giving thanks.
Enter his courts with songs of praise.
Give thanks to him and bless his name. **R.**

Indeed, how good is the Lord,
eternal his merciful love.
He is faithful from age to age. **R.**

SECOND READING   1 Jn 4:7-12

Those who love know God, because God is love.

A reading from the first letter of Saint John
Let us love one another; for love is of God, and he who loves is born of

God and knows God. He who does not love does not know God; for God is love.

In this the love of God was made manifest among us, that God sent his only Son into the world, so that we might live through him. In this is love, not that we loved God but that he loved us and sent his Son to be the expiation for our sins.

If God so loved us, we also ought to love one another. No man has ever seen God; if we love one another, God abides in us and his love is perfected in us.

This is the word of the Lord.

Gospel Acclamation   Jn 15:13

Alleluia, alleluia! (*Lent:* Praise to you, Lord Jesus Christ).
Greater love has no man than this,
that a man lay down his life for his friends,
says the Lord.
Alleluia! (*Lent:* Praise to you, Lord Jesus Christ).

GOSPEL   Mt 19:3-6

Christ teaches that the marriage bond comes from God and is indissoluble.

A reading from the holy Gospel according to Matthew
Some Pharisees came up to Jesus and tested him by asking, "Is it lawful to divorce one's wife for any cause?"

He answered, "Have you not read that he who made them from the beginning made them male and female, and said, "For this reason a man shall leave his father and mother and be joined to his wife, and the two shall become one."

"So they are no longer two but one. What therefore God has joined together, let no man put asunder."

This is the Gospel of the Lord.

9. BUILDING ON ROCK

FIRST READING   Gen 2:18-24

In and through marriage, God intends man and woman to be companions and
helpers to one another, so that in a sense they are no longer two but one.

A reading from the book of Genesis

Then the Lord God said:

"It is not good that the man should be alone; I will make him a helper
fit for him." So out of the ground the Lord God formed every beast of the
field and every bird of the air, and brought them to the man to see what
he would call them; and whatever the man called every living creature,
that was its name.

The man gave names to all cattle, and to the birds of the air, and to
every beast of the field; but for the man there was not found a helper fit
for him. So the Lord God caused a deep sleep to fall upon the man, and
while he slept took one of his ribs and closed up its place with flesh; and
the rib which the Lord God had taken from the man he made into a woman
and brought her to the man. Then the man said, "This at last is bone of my
bones and flesh of my flesh; she shall be called Woman, because she was
taken out of Man."

Therefore a man leaves his father and his mother and cleaves to his
wife, and they become one flesh.

This is the word of the Lord.

Responsorial Psalm   Ps 61(62):2-3,8,11-13

Response: In God alone is my soul at rest.

In God alone is my soul at rest;
my help comes from him.
He alone is my rock, my stronghold,
my fortress: I stand firm. **R.**

Take refuge in God all you people;
trust him at all times.
Pour out your hearts before him
for God is our refuge. **R.**

Do not put your trust in oppression

nor vain hopes of plunder.
Do not set your heart on riches
even when they increase. **R**.

For God has said only one thing:
only two do I know:
that to God alone belongs power
and to you, Lord, love. **R.**

SECOND READING   1 Jn 3:18-24

Christ's great commandment is the commandment to love one another. However,
it is not enough to love in word; we must also love in deed.

A reading from the first letter of Saint John

Little children, let us not love in word or speech but in deed and in truth.

By this we shall know that we are of the truth, and reassure our hearts
before him whenever our hearts condemn us; for God is greater than our
hearts, and he knows everything.

Beloved, if our hearts do not condemn us, we have confidence before
God; and we receive from him whatever we ask, because we keep his
commandments and do what pleases him.

And this is his commandment, that we should believe in the name of
his Son Jesus Christ and love one another, just as he has commanded us.
All who keep his commandments abide in him, and he in them. And by
this we know that he abides in us, by the Spirit which he has given us.

This is the word of the Lord.

Gospel Acclamation   Jn 15:12

Alleluia, alleluia! (*Lent:* Praise to you, Lord Jesus Christ).
This is my commandment,
that you love one another as I have loved you,
says the Lord.
Alleluia! (*Lent:* Praise to you, Lord Jesus Christ).

GOSPEL   Mt 7:21,24-27

*Christ made a wonderful promise to those who are not satisfied merely to listen
to his teaching but who actually carry it out.*

A reading from the holy Gospel according to Matthew
Jesus said to his disciples:
"Not every one who says to me, 'Lord, Lord,' shall enter the kingdom
of heaven, but he who does the will of my Father who is in heaven.
"Every one then who hears these words of mine and does them will be
like a wise man who built his house upon the rock; and the rain fell, and
the floods came, and the winds blew and beat upon that house, but it did
not fall, because it had been founded on the rock.
"And every one who hears these words of mine and does not do them
will be like a foolish man who built his house upon the sand; and the rain
fell, and the floods came, and the winds blew and beat against that house,
and it fell; and great was the fall of it."
This is the Gospel of the Lord.

10. THE BOND OF LOVE

FIRST READING   Sir 6:6-12,14-15

*There is a false friend and a true friend. A false friend is worthless; a true friend
is a treasure.*

A reading from the book of Sirach
Let those that are at peace with you be many,
but let your advisers be one in a thousand.
When you gain a friend, gain him through testing,
and do not trust him hastily.
For there is a friend who is such at his own convenience,
but will not stand by you in your day of trouble.
And there is a friend who changes into an enemy,
and will disclose a quarrel to your disgrace.
And there is a friend who is a table companion,
but will not stand by you in your day of trouble.
In your prosperity he will make himself your equal,
and be bold with your servants;

but if you are brought low he will turn against you,
and will hide himself from your presence.
A faithful friend is a sturdy shelter:
he that has found one has found a treasure.
There is nothing so precious as a faithful friend,
and no scales can measure his excellence.
    This is the word of the Lord.

Responsorial Psalm   Ps 127(128):1-6

Response: Blessed are those who fear the Lord and walk in his ways.

O blessed are those who fear the Lord
and walk in his ways.
By the labour of your hands you shall eat;
you will be happy and prosper. **R**.

Your wife like a fruitful vine
in the heart of your house;
Your children like shoots of the olive,
around your table. **R**.

Indeed thus shall be blessed
the man who fears the Lord.
May the Lord bless you from Sion
all the days of your life. **R**.

SECOND READING   Gal 5:13-14,18,22-23

The whole of God's law can be summed up in the commandment to love.
However, it is only through the grace of the Holy Spirit that we can love properly.

A reading from the letter of St Paul to the Galatians
You were called to freedom, brethren; only do not use your freedom as
an opportunity for the flesh, but through love be servants of one another.
For the whole law is fulfilled in one word, "You shall love your neighbour
as yourself."
    If you are led by the Spirit you are not under the law. The fruit of the
Spirit is love, joy, peace, patience, kindness, goodness, faithfulness,
gentleness, self-control; against such there is no law.
    This is the word of the Lord.

Gospel Acclamation   1 Jn 4:12

Alleluia, alleluia! (*Lent:* Praise to you, Lord Jesus Christ).
If we love one another,
God abides in us
and his love is perfected in us.
Alleluia! (*Lent:* Praise to you, Lord Jesus Christ).

GOSPEL   Mt 19:3-6

Christ teaches that the marriage bond comes from God and is indissoluble.

A reading from the holy Gospel according to Matthew
Some Pharisees came up to Jesus and tested him by asking, "Is it lawful
to divorce one's wife for any cause?"
He answered, "Have you not read that he who made them from the
beginning made them male and female, and said, "For this reason a man
shall leave his father and mother and be joined to his wife, and the two
shall become one."
"So they are no longer two but one. What therefore God has joined
together, let no man put asunder."
This is the Gospel of the Lord.

ALTERNATIVE GOSPEL   Mk 10:6-9

A reading from the holy Gospel according to Mark
Jesus said:
"From the beginning of creation, 'God made them male and female.'
'For this reason a man shall leave his father and mother and be joined to
his wife, and the two shall become one.' So they are no longer two but one.
What therefore God has joined together, let not man put asunder."
This is the Gospel of the Lord.

11. IT'S NOT GOOD TO BE ALONE

FIRST READING   Gen 2:18-24

In and through marriage, God intends man and woman to be companions and helpers to one another, so that in a sense they are no longer two but one.

A reading from the book of Genesis

Then the Lord God said:

"It is not good that the man should be alone; I will make him a helper fit for him." So out of the ground the Lord God formed every beast of the field and every bird of the air, and brought them to the man to see what he would call them; and whatever the man called every living creature, that was its name.

The man gave names to all cattle, and to the birds of the air, and to every beast of the field; but for the man there was not found a helper fit for him. So the Lord God caused a deep sleep to fall upon the man, and while he slept took one of his ribs and closed up its place with flesh; and the rib which the Lord God had taken from the man he made into a woman and brought her to the man. Then the man said, "This at last is bone of my bones and flesh of my flesh; she shall be called Woman, because she was taken out of Man."

Therefore a man leaves his father and his mother and cleaves to his wife, and they become one flesh.

This is the word of the Lord.

Responsorial Psalm   Ps 144 (145):8-11,14,17-18

Response: The Lord is compassionate to all his creatures.

The Lord is kind and full of compassion,
slow to anger, abounding in love.
How good is the Lord to all,
compassionate to all his creatures. **R.**

All your creatures shall thank you, O Lord,
and your fiends shall repeat their blessing.
They shall speak of the glory of your reign
and declare your might, O God. **R.**

The Lord is faithful in all his words
and loving in all his deeds.
The Lord supports all who fall
and raises all who are bowed down. **R.**

The Lord is just in all his ways
and loving in all his deeds.
He is close to all who call him,
who call on him from their hearts. **R.**

SECOND READING   1 Jn 4:7-12

Those who love know God, because God is love.

A reading from the first letter of St John

Let us love one another; for love is of God, and he who loves is born of God and knows God. He who does not love does not know God; for God is love.

In this the love of God was made manifest among us, that God sent his only Son into the world, so that we might live through him. In this is love, not that we loved God but that he loved us and sent his Son to be the expiation for our sins.

If God so loved us, we also ought to love one another. No man has ever seen God; if we love one another, God abides in us and his love is perfected in us.

This is the word of the Lord.

Gospel Acclamation   Jn 13:34

Alleluia, alleluia! (*Lent:* Praise to you, Lord Jesus Christ).
A new commandment I give to you,
that you love one another,
even as I have loved you,
says the Lord.
Alleluia! (*Lent:* Praise to you, Lord Jesus Christ).

GOSPEL   Jn 15:9-12

Christ urges his disciples to love one another as he has loved them.

A reading from the holy Gospel according to John

Jesus said to his disciples:

"As the Father has loved me, so have I loved you; abide in my love. If you keep my commandments, you will abide in my love, just as I have kept my Father's commandments and abide in his love. These things I have spoken to you, that my joy may be in you, and that your joy may be full.

This is my commandment, that you love one another as I have loved you."

This is the Gospel of the Lord.

12. WEEDS AMONG THE WHEAT

FIRST READING   Song 2:10-14,15;8:6-7

This is a poem which sings the praises of love.

A reading from the Song of Songs
My beloved speaks and says to me:
"Arise, my love, my fair one, and come away;
for lo, the winter is past,
the rain is over and gone.
The flowers appear on the earth,
the time of singing has come,
and the voice of the turtle-dove is heard in our land.
The fig tree puts forth its figs,
and the vines are in blossom;
they give forth fragrance.
Arise, my love, my fair one, and come away.
Let me see your face,
let me hear your voice,
for your voice is sweet,
and your face is comely."
My beloved is mine and I am his. He said to me:
"Set me as a seal upon your heart,
as a seal upon your arm;
for love is strong as death.
Many waters cannot quench love,
neither can floods drown it.
If a man offered for love all the wealth of his house,

it would be utterly scorned."
My beloved is mine and I am his.
This is the word of the Lord.

Note: a dialogue version of this beautiful reading can be found in Liturgy No. 4, p. 85.

Responsorial Psalm   Ps 144(145):8-11,14,17-18

Response: The Lord is compassionate to all his creatures.

The Lord is kind and full of compassion,
slow to anger, abounding in love.
How good is the Lord to all,
compassionate to all his creatures. **R.**

All your creatures shall thank you, O Lord,
and your fiends shall repeat their blessing.
They shall speak of the glory of your reign
and declare your might, O God. **R.**

The Lord is faithful in all his words
and loving in all his deeds.
The Lord supports all who fall
and raises all who are bowed down. **R.**

The Lord is just in all his ways
and loving in all his deeds.
He is close to all who call him,
who call on him from their hearts. **R.**

SECOND READING   1 Cor 13:1-7

No one ever so stressed the importance of love, or described it better, than St Paul.

A reading from the first letter of St Paul to the Corinthians
If I speak in the tongues of man and of angels, but have not love, I am a
noisy gong or a clanging cymbal.
     And if I have prophetic powers, and understand all mysteries and all
knowledge, and if I have all faith, so as to remove mountains, but have
not love, I am nothing.
     If I give away all I have, and if I deliver my body to be burned, but have
not love, I gain nothing.
     Love is patient and kind;

love is not jealous or boastful;
it is not arrogant or rude.
Love does not insist on its own way;
it is not irritable or resentful;
it does not rejoice at wrong but rejoices in the right.
Love bears all things,
believes all things,
hopes all things.
Love never ends.
This is the word of the Lord

Gospel Acclamation   1 Jn 4:7-8

Alleluia, alleluia! (*Lent:* Praise to you, Lord Jesus Christ).
He who loves is born of God
and knows God,
for God is love.
Alleluia! (*Lent:* Praise to you, Lord Jesus Christ).

GOSPEL   Mt 13:24-30

A story about a field in which wheat and weeds grow side by side right up to the
day of the harvest.

A reading from the holy Gospel according to Matthew
Jesus spoke this parable to the people:
"The kingdom of heaven may be compared to a man who sowed good seed in his field; but while men were sleeping, his enemy came and sowed weeds among the wheat, and went away. So when the plants came up and bore grain, then the weeds appeared also. And the servants of the householder came and said to him, "Sir, did you not sow good seed in your field? How then has it weeds?" He said to them, "An enemy has done this."
"The servants said to him, "Then do you want us to go and gather them?" But he said, 'No; lest in gathering the weeds you root up the wheat along with them. Let both grow together until the harvest; and at harvest time I will tell the reapers, Gather the weeds first and bind them in bundles to be burned, but gather the wheat into my barn.'"
This is the Gospel of the Lord.

ALTERNATIVE GOSPEL   Jn 13:34-35

Christ urges his disciples to love one another as he has loved them.

A reading from the holy Gospel according to John

Jesus said to his disciples:

"A new commandment I give to you, that you love one another; even as I have loved you, that you also love one another.

"By this all men will know that you are my disciples, if you have love for one another."

This is the Gospel of the Lord

13. FOUR REQUIREMENTS

FIRST READING   Sir 6:6-12,14-15

There is a false friend and a true friend. A false friend is worthless; a true friend is a treasure.

A reading from the book of Sirach

Let those that are at peace with you be many,

but let your advisers be one in a thousand.

When you gain a friend, gain him through testing,

and do not trust him hastily.

For there is a friend who is such at his own convenience,

but will not stand by you in your day of trouble.

And there is a friend who changes into an enemy,

and will disclose a quarrel to your disgrace.

And there is a friend who is a table companion,

but will not stand by you in your day of trouble.

In your prosperity he will make himself your equal,

and be bold with your servants;

but if you are brought low he will turn against you,

and will hide himself from your presence.

A faithful friend is a sturdy shelter:

he that has found one has found a treasure.

There is nothing so precious as a faithful friend,

and no scales can measure his excellence.

This is the word of the Lord.

Responsorial Psalm   Ps 26(27):1,4,10,13,14

Response: The Lord is my light and my help.

The Lord is my light and my help;
whom shall I fear?
The Lord is the stronghold of my life;
before whom shall I shrink? **R**.

There is one thing I ask of the Lord,
for this I long,
to live in the house of the Lord
all the days of my life. **R**.

Do not abandon or forsake me,
O God my help.
Though father and mother forsake me,
the Lord will receive me. **R**.

I am sure I shall see the Lord's goodness
in the land of the living.
Hope in him, hold firm and take heart.
Hope in the Lord. **R**.

SECOND READING   1 Cor 13:1-7

No one has ever so stressed the importance of love, or described it better, than St Paul.

A reading from the first letter of St Paul to the Corinthians
If I speak in the tongues of men and of angels, but have not love, I am a noisy gong or a clanging cymbal.

And if I have prophetic powers, and understand all mysteries and all knowledge, and if I have all faith, so as to remove mountains, but have not love, I am nothing.

If I give away all I have, and if I deliver my body to be burned, but have not love, I gain nothing.

Love is patient and kind;
love is not jealous or boastful;
it is not arrogant or rude.
Love does not insist on its own way;
it is not irritable or resentful;
it does not rejoice at wrong, but rejoices in the right.

Love bears all things,
believes all things,
hopes all things.
Love never ends.
This is the word of the Lord.

Gospel Acclamation   1 Jn 3:18

Alleluia, alleluia! (*Lent:* Praise to you, Lord Jesus Christ).
Let us not love in word or speech
but in deed and in truth.
Alleluia! (*Lent:* Praise to you, Lord Jesus Christ).

GOSPEL   Mk 10:6-9

Christ teaches that the marriage bond comes from God and is indissoluble.

A reading from the holy Gospel according to Mark
Jesus said:
"From the beginning of creation, 'God made them male and female.'
'For this reason a man shall leave his father and mother and be joined to
his wife, and the two shall become one.' So they are no longer two but one.
What therefore God has joined together, let not man put asunder."
This is the Gospel of the Lord.

14. CROSSING THE BRIDGE

FIRST READING   Gen 2:18-24

In and through marriage, God intends man and woman to be companions and
helpers to one another, so that in a sense they are no longer two but one.

A reading from the book of Genesis
Then the Lord God said:
"It is not good that the man should be alone; I will make him a helper
fit for him." So out of the ground the Lord God formed every beast of the
field and every bird of the air, and brought them to the man to see what
he would call them; and whatever the man called every living creature,
that was its name.

The man gave names to all cattle, and to the birds of the air, and to every beast of the field; but for the man there was not found a helper fit for him. So the Lord God caused a deep sleep to fall upon the man, and while he slept took one of his ribs and closed up its place with flesh; and the rib which the Lord God had taken from the man he made into a woman and brought her to the man. Then the man said, "This at last is bone of my bones and flesh of my flesh; she shall be called Woman, because she was taken out of Man."

Therefore a man leaves his father and his mother and cleaves to his wife, and they become one flesh.

This is the word of the Lord.

Responsorial Psalm   Ps 32(33):12-15,18-22

Response: May your love be upon us, O Lord,
as we place all our hope in you.

They are happy, whose God is the Lord,
the people he has chosen as his own.
From the heavens the Lord looks forth,
he sees all the children of men. **R.**

From the place where he dwells he gazes
on all the dwellers on the earth,
he who shapes the hearts of them all
and considers all their deeds. **R.**

The Lord looks on those who revere him,
on those who hope in his love,
to rescue their souls from death,
to keep them alive in famine. **R.**

Our soul is waiting for the Lord.
The Lord is our help and our shield.
In him do our hearts find joy.
We trust in his holy name. **R.**

SECOND READING   1 Cor 13:1-7

No one ever so stressed the importance of love, or described it better, than St Paul.

A reading from the first letter of St Paul to the Corinthians
If I speak in the tongues of men and of angels, but have not love, I am a

noisy gong or a clanging cymbal.

And if I have prophetic powers, and understand all mysteries and all knowledge, and if I have all faith, so as to remove mountains, but have not love, I am nothing.

If I give away all I have, and if I deliver my body to be burned, but have not love, I gain nothing.

Love is patient and kind;
love is not jealous or boastful;
it is not arrogant or rude.
Love does not insist on its own way;
it is not irritable or resentful;
it does not rejoice at wrong, but rejoices in the right.
Love bears all things,
believes all things,
hopes all things.
Love never ends.
This is the word of the Lord.

Gospel Acclamation   Jn 13:35

Alleluia, alleluia! (*Lent:* Praise to you, Lord Jesus Christ).
By this all men will know that you are my disciples,
if you have love for one another,
says the Lord.
Alleluia! (*Lent:* Praise to you, Lord Jesus Christ).

GOSPEL   Jn 13:34-35

Christ urges his disciples to love one another as he has loved them.

A reading from the holy Gospel according to John
Jesus said to his disciples:

"A new commandment I give to you, that you love one another; even as I have loved you, that you also love one another.

"By this all men will know that you are my disciples, if you have love for one another."

This is the Gospel of the Lord.

15. REMAINING FAITHFUL

FIRST READING   Is 54:4-5,9-10

God has made an everlasting covenant with us. Therefore there is no need to be
anxious or fearful.

A reading from the prophet Isaiah

"Fear not, for you will not be ashamed;
be not confounded, for you will not be put to shame.
For your Maker is your husband,
the Lord of hosts is his name;
and the Holy One of Israel is your Redeemer,
the God of the whole earth he is called.
With everlasting love I will have compassion on you,
says the Lord, your Redeemer.
For this is like the days of Noah to me:
as I swore that the waters of Noah
should no more go over the earth,
so I have sworn that I will not be angry with you
and will not rebuke you.
For the mountains may depart
and the hills be removed,
but my steadfast love shall not depart from you,
and my covenant of peace shall not be removed,
says the Lord, who has compassion on you.
This is the word of the Lord.

Responsorial Psalm   Ps 137(138):1-3,6-7

Response: Your love, O Lord, is eternal.

I thank you, Lord, with all my heart,
you have heard the words of my mouth.
Before the angels I will bless you.
I will adore before your holy temple. **R.**

I thank you for your faithfulness and love
which excel all we ever knew of you.
On the day I called, you answered;
you increased the strength of my soul. **R.**

The Lord is high yet he looks on the lowly
and the haughty he knows from afar.
Though I walk in the midst of affliction
you give me life and frustrate my foes. **R.**

You stretch out your hand and save me,
your hand will do all things for me.
Your love, O Lord, is eternal,
discard not the work of your hands. **R.**

SECOND READING   Rom 8:31-35,37-39

Because God loves us and always takes our side, we are able to overcome every
kind of trial and suffering.

A reading from the letter of St Paul to the Romans
If God is for us, who is against us? He who did not spare his own Son but
gave him up for us all, will he not also give us all things with him? Who
shall bring any charge against God's elect? It is God who justifies; who
is to condemn? Is it Christ Jesus, who died, yes, who was raised from the
dead, who is at the right hand of God, who indeed intercedes for us?

Who shall separate us from the love of Christ? Shall tribulation, or
distress, or persecution, or famine, or nakedness, or peril, or sword? No,
in all these things we are more than conquerors through him who loved
us. For I am sure that neither death, nor life, nor angels, nor principalities,
nor things present, nor things to come, nor powers, nor height, nor depth,
nor anything else in all creation, will be able to separate us from the love
of God in Christ Jesus our Lord.

This is the word of the Lord.

Gospel Acclamation   1 Jn 4:7

Alleluia, alleluia! (*Lent:* Praise to you, Lord Jesus Christ).
Let us love one another;
for love is of God,
and he who loves is born of God
and knows God.
Alleluia! (*Lent:* Praise to you, Lord Jesus Christ).

GOSPEL   Jn 15:9-12

Christ urges his disciples to love one another as he has loved them.

A reading from the holy Gospel according to John
Jesus said to his disciples:

"As the Father has loved me, so have I loved you; abide in my love.
If you keep my commandments, you will abide in my love, just as I have
kept my Father's commandments and abide in his love. These things I
have spoken to you, that my joy may be in you, and that your joy may be
full.

"This is my commandment, that you love one another as I have loved
you."

This is the Gospel of the Lord.

16. THE LAMP STILL BURNS

FIRST READING   Sir 6:6-12,14-15

There is a false friend and a true friend. A false friend is worthless; a true friend
is a treasure.

A reading from the book of Sirach
Let those that are at peace with you be many,
but let your advisers be one in a thousand.
When you gain a friend, gain him through testing,
and do not trust him hastily.
For there is a friend who is such at his own convenience,
but will not stand by you in your day of trouble.
And there is a friend who changes into an enemy,
and will disclose a quarrel to your disgrace,
And there is a friend who is a table companion,
but will not stand by you in your day of trouble.
In your prosperity he will make himself your equal,
and be bold with your servants;
but if you are brought low he will turn against you,
and will hide himself from your presence.
A faithful friend is a sturdy shelter:
he that has found one has found a treasure.

There is nothing so precious as a faithful friend,
and no scales can measure his excellence.
This is the word of the Lord.

Responsorial Psalm   Ps 26(27):1,4,10,13,14

Response: The Lord is my light and my help.

The Lord is my light and my help;
whom shall I fear?
The Lord is the stronghold of my life;
before whom shall I shrink? **R.**

There is one thing I ask of the Lord,
for this I long,
to live in the house of the Lord
all the days of my life. **R.**

Do not abandon or forsake me,
O God my help.
Though father and mother forsake me,
the Lord will receive me. **R.**

I am sure I shall see the Lord's goodness
in the land of the living.
Hope in him, hold firm and take heart.
Hope in the Lord. **R.**

SECOND READING   1 Jn 2:7-11

To love is to walk in the light; not to love is to walk in darkness.

A reading from the first letter of John

Beloved, I am writing you no new commandment, but an old commandment which you had from the beginning; the old commandment is the
word which you have heard.

Yet I am writing you a new commandment, which is true in him and
in you, because the darkness is passing away and the true light is already
shining.

He who says he is in the light and hates his brother is in the darkness
still. He who loves his brother abides in the light, and in it there is no cause
for stumbling. But he who hates his brother is in the darkness and walks

in the darkness, and does not know where he is going, because the
darkness has blinded his eyes.

This is the word of the Lord.

Gospel Acclamation   1 Jn 4:7-8

Alleluia, alleluia! (*Lent:* Praise to you, Lord Jesus Christ).
He who loves is born of God
and knows God,
for God is love.
Alleluia! (*Lent:* Praise to you, Lord Jesus Christ).

GOSPEL   Jn 13:34-35

Christ urges his disciples to love one another as he has loved them.

A reading from the holy Gospel according to John
Jesus said to his disciples:

"A new commandment I give to you, that you love one another; even
as I have loved you, that you also love one another.

"By this all men will know that you are my disciples, if you have love
for one another."

This is the Gospel of the Lord.

17. STILL ON THE CHOSEN ROAD

FIRST READING   Gen 1:26-28,31

God made man and woman for one another. The bond of marriage means that in
a sense they are no longer two but one.

A reading from the book of Genesis
Then God said:

"Let us make man in our image, after our likeness; and let them have
dominion over the fish of the sea, and over the birds of the air, and over
the cattle, and over all the earth, and over every creeping thing that creeps
upon the earth."

So God created man in his own image, in the image of God he created
him; male and female he created them. And God blessed them, and God

said to them, "Be fruitful and multiply, and fill the earth and subdue it; and have dominion over the fish of the sea and over the birds of the air and over every living thing that moves upon the earth."

And God saw everything that he had made, and behold it was very good.

This is the word of the Lord.

Responsorial Psalm   Ps 102(103): 8,10-14,17-18

Response: The Lord is compassion and love.

The Lord is compassion and love,
slow to anger and rich in mercy.
He does not treat us according to our sins
nor repay us according to our faults. **R.**

For as the heavens are high above the earth
so strong is his love for those who fear him.
As far as the east is from the west
so far does he remove our sins. **R.**

As a father has compassion on his children,
the Lord has pity on those who fear him;
for he knows of what we are made,
he remembers that we are dust. **R.**

The love of the Lord is everlasting
upon those who fear him;
his justice reaches out to children's children
when they keep his covenant in truth. **R.**

SECOND READING   Phil 4:4-9

This reading tells us what we must do if we wish to live in peace with God and with one another.

A reading from the letter of St Paul to the Philippians
Rejoice in the Lord always; again I will say. Rejoice. Let all men know your forbearance. The Lord is at hand. Have no anxiety about anything, but in everything by prayer and supplication with thanksgiving let your request be made known to God. And the peace of God, which passes all understanding, will keep your hearts and your minds in Christ Jesus.

Finally, brethren, whatever is true, whatever is honourable, whatever is just, whatever is pure, whatever is lovely, whatever is gracious, if there is any excellence, if there is anything worthy of praise, think about these things. What you have learned and received and heard and seen in me, do; and the God of peace will be with you.

This is the word of the Lord.

Gospel Acclamation   1 Jn 4:12

Alleluia, alleluia! (*Lent:* Praise to you, Lord Jesus Christ).
If we love one another,
God abides in us
and his love is perfected in us.
Alleluia! (*Lent:* Praise to you, Lord Jesus Christ).

GOSPEL   Jn 13:34-35

Christ urges his disciples to love one another as he has loved them.

A reading from the holy Gospel according to John
Jesus said to his disciples:

"A new commandment I give to you, that you love one another; even as I have loved you, that you also love one another.

"By this all men will know that you are my disciples, if you have love for one another."

This is the Gospel of the Lord.

18. THE BOND STILL HOLDS

FIRST READING   Gen 2:18-24

In and through marriage God intended man and woman to be companions and helpers to one another, so that in a sense they are no longer two but one.

A reading from the book of Genesis
Then the Lord God said:

"It is not good that the man should be alone; I will make him a helper fit for him." So out of the ground the Lord God formed every beast of the field and every bird of the air, and brought them to the man to see what he would call them; and whatever the man called every living creature, that was its name.

The man gave names to all cattle, and to the birds of the air, and to every beast of the field; but for the man there was not found a helper fit for him. So the Lord God caused a deep sleep to fall upon the man, and while he slept took one of his ribs and closed up its place with flesh; and the rib which the Lord God had taken from the man he made into a woman and brought her to the man. Then the man said, "This at last is bone of my bones and flesh of my flesh; she shall be called Woman, because she was taken out of Man."

Therefore a man leaves his father and his mother and cleaves to his wife, and they become one flesh.

This is the word of the Lord.

Responsorial Psalm   Ps 91(92):2-6,13-16

Response: It is good to give thanks to the Lord.

It is good to give thanks to the Lord
to make music to your name, O Most High,
to proclaim your love in the morning
and your truth in the watches of the night. **R**.

Your deeds, O Lord, have made me glad;
for the work of your hands I shout with joy.
O Lord, how great are your works,
how deep are your designs. **R**.

The just will flourish like the palm-tree
and grow like a Lebanon cedar.
Planted in the House of the Lord
they will flourish in the courts of our God. **R**.

Still bearing fruit when they are old,
still full of sap, still green,
to proclaim that the Lord is just;
in him, my rock, there is no wrong. **R**.

SECOND READING   1 Cor 13:1-7

No one ever so stressed the importance of love, or described it better, than St Paul.

A reading from the first letter of St Paul to the Corinthians.
If I speak in the tongues of men and of angels, but have not love, I am a noisy gong or a clanging cymbal.

And if I have prophetic powers, and understand all mysteries and all knowledge, and if I have all faith, so as to remove mountains, but have not love, I am nothing.

If I give away all I have, and if I deliver my body to be burned, but have not love, I gain nothing.

Love is patient and kind;
love is not jealous or boastful;
it is not arrogant or rude.
Love does not insist on its own way;
it is not irritable or resentful;
it does not rejoice at wrong, but rejoices in the right.
Love bears all things,
believes all things,
hopes all things.
Love never ends.
This is the word of the Lord.

Gospel Acclamation   1 Jn 3:18

Alleluia, alleluia! (*Lent:* Praise to you, Lord Jesus Christ).
Let us not love in word or speech
but in deed and in truth.
Alleluia! (*Lent:* Praise to you, Lord Jesus Christ).

GOSPEL   Jn 15:9-12

Christ urges his disciples to love one another as he has loved them.

A reading from the holy Gospel according to John
Jesus said to his disciples:
"As the Father has loved me, so have I loved you; abide in my love. If you keep my commandments, you will abide in my love, just as I have kept my Father's commandments and abide in his love. These things I have spoken to you, that my joy may be in you, and that your joy may be full.

"This is my commandment, that you love one another as I have loved you."

This is the Gospel of the Lord.

Reflections

1. Love Is Well-Being

Some people enter a relationship
with the mentality of a beggar:
they want to receive all the time.
For them to give is to be deprived of something,
and to give without receiving is to be cheated.

But others have a more mature attitude.
They know they need to receive,
because of ourselves we are incomplete.
But they also know they need to give.
For them to give is to be enriched.
In it they discover their own wealth,
and experience a feeling of being alive,
just as a tree does in springtime,
when offering its buds and blossoms to the world.

Love is well-being.
To open one's heart is to begin to live;
to close it is to begin to die.

The love of others for me is a blessing,
and still more is my love for others.

2. Entering the Magic Kingdom

Animals shed their hair;
some even shed their skins.
Trees shed their leaves;
some even shed their barks.
All these do so, of course,
at their own pace
and in the proper season.

And far from suffering deprivation or death,
they are continually renewed.
But try taking these things away from them,
and you will destroy them.

It is much the same with people.
There is no point in forcing them to make sacrifices.
If you take things away from them,
they are impoverished.
But if you can get them to let go of them,
they are enriched.

Just as in the warmth of spring sunshine
the rose begins to open up petal by petal,
so in the warm climate of love,
a human being begins to open up and grow.

People are essentially good,
but this goodness has to be called forth
if they are to enter the magic kingdom of love.

3. Slow Down

Though the stream was in a hurry to reach the plains
nevertheless, it took time to form pools.
Around these pools grass grew;
from them animals quenched their thirst;
within them frogs jumped for joy.

Today people are always rushing.
They seem unable to slow down
and spend time with one another.
No wonder they offer one another so little.
It is hard to drink from a fast-flowing stream.

Friendship is about having time for someone,
spending time with that person,
being present to that person,
so that life can flow from one to the other.

The greatest gift I can give to another person

is the gift of my time.
To give of my time is to give of myself.

If I wish to nourish another person
I must allow the stream of my life
to slow down and form a pool.
From this pool the other will drink.

4. Knowing God

A young disciple who was having doubts
came to the Master and asked:
"Do you believe in God?"
"Yes, I do," the Master answered.
The disciple then asked:
"On what evidence do you believe?"
"I believe in God because I know him,"
came the reply.
"I experience his presence in me
twenty-four hours of every day."
"But how is this possible?"
the disciple demanded.
"When we love, we experience God,
and doubt vanishes like mist before the sun,"
replied the Master.

The disciple thought for a while, then asked:
"How can I achieve this kind of certainty?"
"By acts of love," the Master replied.
"Try to love your neighbours;
love them actively and unceasingly.
And as you learn to love them more and more,
you will become more and more convinced
of the existence of God
and the immortality of the soul.
This has been tested.
This is the true way."

5. Not a Ready-made Garment

Love is not a ready-made garment,
    but a piece of material to be cut and tailored.
It is not a flat ready for occupation,
    but a house to be designed, built, furnished and repaired.

It is not a conquered peak,
    but a daunting ascent with many obstacles and falls
    made in the icy cold or the fierce heat.
It is not a safe anchorage in a harbour of happiness,
    but a voyage on the open sea in storm and tempest.

It is not a triumphant "yes", an affirmation of success,
    a magnificent final chord followed by clapping and cheers,
but "yes" repeated again and again throughout life
    accompanied by "no" repeated as many times, but overcome.

It is not the sudden appearance of a new life,
    perfect from the moment of its birth,
but the flowing of a river from its source,
    sometimes in flood and sometimes only as a trickle of water,
    but always on its way to the infinite sea.

From *The Breath of Love*, by Michel Quoist, published by Gill and Macmillan, and used with permission.

6. When First Love Fades

To the gardener it seemed that winter would never end.
But one morning he went out into his orchard
to find the sun shining, birds singing,
and flowers and blossoms everywhere.
Overnight the world had become a wonderland.
He was intoxicated with joy.

Alas, the magic didn't last.
The blossoms soon faded and fell to the ground.
Grass and weeds rose up and smothered the flowers.
Though saddened, the gardener didn't despair;
the year was young and things were growing.

Then on another morning he went out,
and under the leaves,
he saw tiny apples beginning to take shape.
Once again his heart was filled with joy.

First love is like springtime.
It is a time of wonder and magic,
which banishes the winter of sadness and loneliness.
But it doesn't last.

We pray for N. and N.,
so that when the blossoms fade,
their young love may continue to grow.

God blesses their love
and wants it to bear fruit.

7. Till Love Came

Darkness came down, and then
I doubted all;
And there was no one in the lonely glen
To hear my call.

I doubted God, and I doubted
My secret soul;
The legions of Heaven were routed
And I had no goal.

I doubted Beauty and Love
And wandered forth
A child of despair, to rove
The faithless earth.

And then like an angel she came;
I ceased to rove;
In her heart was a pure white flame
And she was love.

Patrick Kavanagh.

8. Presence and Absence

We have to meet and spend time together
for a bond to form between us.
But physical presence doesn't always
produce the intimacy we long for.
In fact, when people spend all their time together,
real friendship between them becomes difficult.

Presence blinds.
It is a well-known fact
that what we love and admire in our friends
is often clearer to us in their absence.
Hence, separation is necessary if we are to achieve
a deeper union and oneness of life.

But there is danger in separation too.
If we are apart for too long,
and communicate too seldom,
the thread of our friendship
may be stretched to breaking point.
A relationship suffers from neglect
just as surely as a garden does.

For closeness to grow there must be a continuous
interplay between presence and absence.

9. Encountering the Other

A husband and wife can be together
and yet never really encounter one another.
They can live in the same house,
sleep in the same bed,
sit at the same table,
kneel in the same church pew,
exchange many words,
give each other signs of apparent tenderness,
and yet never really meet.
Though living side by side,
they remain separate, lonely creatures,

like shells on a shore.

But they can encounter one another.
In an encounter,
all barriers fall down,
all pretence is set aside;
people open their hearts to one another,
so that life flows from one to the other.
An encounter is a strange and wonderful thing.
When it happens, people are transformed.

Lord, look with love today on N. and N.
Do not condemn them to be alone when together.
Rather, help them to be together when alone.

10. An Unbreakable Bond

Though only two weeks had gone by since the thaw set in,
there wasn't a snowflake to be seen.
That self-same snow,
which had lain so deep,
and which had been reinforced by an arctic frost,
was now only a memory.
It had melted before the sun,
and been washed away by the rain.

But what was this I saw by the side of the road?
A mound of snow!
How come the flakes in this mound had managed to survive
when all the others had vanished?
The explanation was quite simple.
The snow-plough which had pushed them off the road
had formed them into such a tightly-knit unit
that they were able to withstand the best efforts
of sun and rain to obliterate them.

May the Lord in his love
so bind N. and N. together today
that nothing on this earth will separate them.

11. A True Friend

It is a fact that happy marriages result
when the partners are also good friends.
But how do you define what a friend is?

Consider the moon.
When full, it is beautiful.
But it is not always full;
it waxes and wanes.
Nor is it always there.
Frequently you find that
it is there when you don't need it,
and not there when you do need it.
A true friend is not like the moon.

Now consider the stars.
See how they stay with us right through the night,
unfailing, untiring, undemanding,
guiding, inspiring, and watching over us.
The darker the night, the brighter they shine.
If sometimes they are not visible to us,
the fault is not theirs —
clouds have got in the way.
But they are still there,
straining to shine on us.

A true friend is like a star.
A true friend is a star.

12. Friendship

It is a fact that happy marriages result
when the partners are also good friends.
But how do you define what friendship is?
Here is Kahlil Gibran's answer:

"Your friend is your needs answered.
He is your field which you sow with love
and reap with thanksgiving.

"Let your best be for your friend.
If he must know the ebb of your tide,
let him know its flood also.
For what is your friend that you should
seek him with hours to kill?
Seek him always with hours to live.
For it is his to fill your need,
but not your emptiness.

"And in the sweetness of friendship
let there be laughter,
and sharing of pleasures.
For in the dew of little things
the heart finds its morning and is refreshed."

From *The Prophet*, by Kahlil Gibran, published by William Heinemann Ltd, and used with permission.

13. Spaces

N. and N. you are together now,
"and together you shall be for ever more,
But let there be spaces in your togetherness,
and let the winds of heaven dance between you.

Love one another, but make not a bond of love:
let it rather be a moving sea
between the shores of your souls.

Fill each other's cup
but drink not from the same cup.
Give one another of your bread
but eat not from the same loaf.

Sing and dance together and be joyous,
but let each one of you be alone,
even as the strings of a lute are alone
though they quiver with the same music.

Give your hearts,
but not into each other's keeping.

For only the hand of Life can contain your hearts.

And stand together yet not too near together;
for the pillars of the temple stand apart,
and the oak tree and the cypress
grow not in each other's shadow."

From *The Prophet*, by Kahlil Gibran, published by William Heinemann Ltd, and used with
permission.

14. Promises to Keep

Promises are easy to make but hard to keep. It does not take much to side-
track us. And we are just as likely to be side-tracked by the good as by the
bad, as this lovely poem says.

Whose woods these are I hardly know
His house is in the village though;
He will not see me stopping here
To watch his woods fill up with snow.

My little horse must think it queer
To stop without a farm house near;
Between the woods and frozen lake
The darkest evening of the year.

He gives his harness bells a shake
To ask if there is some mistake;
The only other sound is the sweep
Of easy wind and downy flake.

The woods are lovely, dark and deep;
But I have promises to keep,
And miles to go before I sleep,
And miles to be before I sleep.

Robert Frost, *Woods in Winter*.

15. Faithfulness

Being faithful is not
    never losing one's way,
    never fighting,
    never falling.
It is always getting up and going on again.
It is wanting to follow to the end the route
    that you have decided on and mapped out together.

It is trusting each other,
    beyond the darkness and shadows.
It is supporting one another,
    beyond the falls and bruises.
It is having faith in the total power of God's Love,
    beyond human love itself.

Faithfulness is very often the faithfulness of Jesus,
    who was nailed to the cross,
    his body and heart tortured by man's lack of faithfulness,
    alone,
    abandoned,
    betrayed,
but who remained faithful to death,
giving and forgiving,
offering his life for us
and saving Love for ever.

16. Thank You

I love you
not only for what you are,
but for what I am when I am with you.

I love you
not only for what you have made of yourself,
but for what you are making of me.

I love you
for the part of me that you bring out;
for passing over the many foolish and weak things
you find in me,
and for drawing out into the light
all the beautiful things only you could find in me.

You have done more for me than any creed.
You have made me feel my own goodness.

And all this you have done
with your touch,
with your words,
with yourself.
Thank you.

Anonymous

17. Living in the Present

Many people allow life to slip away, wishing and waiting for a better future that never comes. According to Emerson they would be better advised to make the most of the opportunities and blessings that come to them every day through those with whom they share their lives. He says:

Sadly, I am often tempted to postpone life.
I refuse sympathy and intimacy with people,
as if expecting a better intimacy to come.
But from where is it going to come
and when?

I am thirty-four years old.
Already my friends and fellow workers
are dying from me.
I rarely see new people approaching me.
I am too old to bother about fashion;
too old to expect the patronage of the powerful.

Let me, therefore, suck the sweetness
of those affections that grow near me,
and which divine Providence offers me.

I pluck golden fruit from rare meetings with wise men.
In the intervals I can well abide alone,
and the fruit of my own tree
will have a better flavour.

The days come and go like muffled figures
sent from a distant friendly land.
If we do not use the gifts they bring,
they carry them as silently away.

Ralph Waldo Emerson.